Listening First

Ten practice tests for the
Cambridge B2 First

Michael Macdonald

PROSPERITY EDUCATION

PROSPERITY EDUCATION
www.prosperityeducation.net

Registered offices: Sherlock Close, Cambridge
CB3 0HP, United Kingdom

© Prosperity Education Ltd. 2019

First published 2019

ISBN: 978-1-79-556211-9

Manufactured on demand by Kindle Direct Publishing.

This publication is in copyright. Subject to statutory exception
and to the provisions of relevant collective licensing agreements,
no reproduction of any part may take place without the written
permission of Prosperity Education.

'Use of English', Cambridge B2 First' and 'FCE' are brands
belonging to The Chancellor, Masters and Scholars of the
University of Cambridge and are not associated with
Prosperity Education or its apps, FCE Academy and CAE Academy,
and related products.

The moral rights of the author have been asserted in accordance with
the Copyright, Designs and Patents Act 1988.

For further information and resources, visit:
www.prosperityeducation.net

To infinity and beyond.

Contents

Introduction	2
About the B2 First Listening	3
Prosperity Education	4
Test 1	5
Test 2	15
Test 3	25
Test 4	35
Test 5	45
Test 6	55
Test 7	65
Test 8	75
Test 9	85
Test 10	95
Answer keys	105
Transcript – Test 1	115
Transcript – Test 2	120
Transcript – Test 3	125
Transcript – Test 4	130
Transcript – Test 5	135
Transcript – Test 6	140
Transcript – Test 7	145
Transcript – Test 8	150
Transcript – Test 9	155
Transcript – Test 10	160
How to download the audio	166

Introduction

Welcome to this edition of sample tests for the Cambridge B2 First Listening, which has been written to closely replicate the Cambridge exam experience and has undergone rigorous expert and peer review. It comprises ten B2 First Listening tests, 300 individual assessments with answer keys, audio transcripts, write-in answer sheets and a marking scheme, providing a large bank of high-quality, test-practice material for candidates.

The accompanying audio files to this resource are available to download from the Prosperity Education website (see the end of this book for instructions). The content in this volume is also available in the FCE Academy Listening mobile app, part of a suite of critically acclaimed, test-practice learning tools geared towards the Cambridge B2 First and C1 Advanced Use of English and Listening exams.

You or your students, if you are a teacher, will hopefully enjoy the wide range of recordings and benefit from the repetitive practice, something that is key to preparing for this part of the B2 First (FCE) examination.

For me, having prepared many students for this and other Cambridge exams, pre- and post-2015, when the specification changed, this is, for many, the section that poses a significant challenge. Without there being much support available by way of quality practice material, students struggle to gain the necessary levels of confidence in the Listening section prior to sitting the exam. Therefore, in my classes, after studying and working through the core knowledge required, we drill, drill and drill exercises in preparation for the exams.

I hope that you will find this resource a useful study aid, and I wish you all the best in preparing for the exam.

Michael Macdonald
Madrid, 2019

About the B2 First Listening

The Cambridge English B2 First (FCE) examination is a timed assessment, with approximately 40 minutes assigned to the Listening section, which is worth 20% of the available grade and comprises 30 individual assessments.

The Listening section of the examination tests candidates' abilities to follow a diverse range of spoken English, and to understand the speakers' personal opinions and attitudes, specific information being conveyed and also general meaning of lengthier monologues. It is broken down in to four parts with one mark awarded to each correct answer:

- Part 1 contains eight short recordings of individuals speaking in eight different situations. Each recording is followed by a multiple-choice question.

- Part 2 is a longer recording of an individual speaking about a specific topic. In each of the ten sentences that follow, a word or short phrase has been removed.

- Part 3 contains five short recordings of individuals speaking about a common subject. Each recording is followed by a multiple-choice question.

- Part 4 is a longer recording of an individual speaking about a specific topic. There follows seven multiple-choice questions.

In the exam, candidates will hear each recording twice and will be given time to read the questions before the recording is played. Candidates are encouraged to take notes during the recordings, before submitting their answers in a separate answer sheet at the end of the exam.

For more information, visit the Cambridge Assessment English website.

Prosperity Education

Exam-quality test practice for the Cambridge B2 First (FCE) and C1 Advanced (CAE) – written, reviewed and produced by English-exam-preparation experts.

Apps

 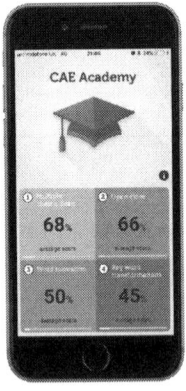  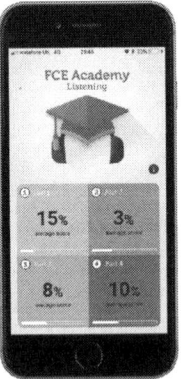

The Academy apps: Thousands of Cambridge B2 First (FCE) and C1 Advanced (CAE) Use of English and Listening exercises, available on GooglePlay and the AppStore. Users can try 'lite' versions of all apps for free.

Books

Practice tests for the Cambridge B2 First (FCE) and C1 Advanced (CAE), Use of English and Listening, complete with full answer keys, transcripts and audio; written by Michael Macdonald and available on Amazon.

Visit www.prosperityeducation.net to read our user reviews, and follow us on Facebook and Twitter for free Cambridge-exam resources, information on forthcoming publications, and updates and promotions.

An unlimited, 50% discount is provided with this resource, redeemable against the FCE Academy app.

Cambridge B2 First Listening

Test 1

Cambridge B2 First Listening

Part 1   Test 1

Audio track: FCE_Listening_1_1.mp3

You will hear people speaking in eight different situations. For questions 1–8, select the best answer A, B, or C. Read the question carefully before playing the audio. In the exam, you will have the opportunity to listen to each recording twice.

1. You hear two people talking about the college canteen. How do they disagree?

    A   The quality of the food

    B   The price of the coffee

    C   The friendliness of the staff

2. You hear a woman talking about life skills. Where does she think the most valuable lessons are learned?

    A   At home

    B   At university

    C   Playing sports

3. You hear an announcement at the airport. What problem is being explained?

    A   Longer queues than usual

    B   Departing flights will be delayed

    C   Arriving flights will be delayed

4. You hear a woman presenting on a TV show. What is she talking about?

    A   Where to buy a present

    B   How to make a cake

    C   How to shop for food

Cambridge B2 First Listening

Part 1   Cont.   Test 1

Audio track: FCE_Listening_1_1.mp3

5 You hear two students talking about a teacher. How does the boy feel?

    A He is really keen to impress the teacher

    B He is worried the teacher doesn't like him

    C He doesn't have confidence in the teacher

6 You hear a football commentary on the radio. What is the reporter doing?

    A Describing how he felt about the match

    B Appreciating some of the players' skills during the match

    C Explaining why the match was cancelled

7 You overhear two friends who have just been to the cinema. What do they agree on?

    A The cinema is still the best form of entertainment

    B The entrance fee is too high

    C The movie was fantastic

8 You hear a man speaking on a telephone. What is he trying to do?

    A Buy a ticket for the train

    B Book a holiday

    C Complain about something

Cambridge B2 First Listening

Part 2 — **Test 1**

Audio track: FCE_Listening_1_2.mp3

You will hear Dom Marcus, a professional actor, talking about his career. For questions 9–18, complete the sentence with a word or short phrase (a maximum of three words). Read the question carefully before playing the audio. In the exam, you will have the opportunity to listen to each recording twice.

The activity he was most interested in at school was [9]. It was when a [10] visited the school that he first became interested in acting.

He found [11] the most challenging thing at drama college. Dom got his lucky break working on a [12] for dog food. Social events are important for [13] and really help to get new jobs. An actor must be prepared for [14] and rejection. Sometimes he has to reject work because he is [15] to accept it. His daughter helps him to understand [16] so that he can use it effectively.

Dom's least favourite type of work is acting in [17], due to the repetitive and slow-moving nature of the production process. Dom says a young actor must know his or her [18].

Cambridge B2 First Listening

Part 3 — Test 1

Audio track: FCE_Listening_1_3.mp3

You will hear five different people talking about their student days. For questions 19–23, select from the list (A–H) what each person speaks about. There are three extra statements which you do not have to use. Read the question carefully before playing the audio. In the exam, you will have the opportunity to listen to each recording twice.

Which person speaks about:

A   hating the late night parties

B   finding it hard to focus at first

C   being older than the other students

D   becoming aware of the wider world

E   it helping them to make important changes

F   getting into trouble for cheating

G   missing the support of their family

H   struggling financially

Speaker 1		19
Speaker 2		20
Speaker 3		21
Speaker 4		22
Speaker 5		23

Cambridge B2 First Listening

Part 4

Test 1

Audio track: FCE_Listening_1_4.mp3

You will hear an interview with a man called Raymond Osman, who works as a chiropractor in Madrid. For questions 24–30, select the best answer A, B, or C. Read the question carefully before playing the audio. In the exam, you will have the opportunity to listen to each recording twice.

24 How do Raymond's parents feel about him becoming a chiropractor?

   A Surprised

   B Proud

   C Ashamed

25 On living in Spain, Raymond says:

   A He misses England more than his wife does.

   B His wife misses England more than he does.

   C His parents want him to move to Barcelona.

26 Raymond lives in Spain because:

   A there is a high demand for his services there

   B his parents live there

   C his wife is Spanish

27 Which aspect of his job does Raymond enjoy the most?

   A Studying new techniques

   B Rehabilitating professional athletes

   C Speaking at conferences

Cambridge B2 First Listening

Part 4   **Cont.**   **Test 1**

Audio track: FCE_Listening_1_4.mp3

28 He believes most people suffer health problems because:

     A they don't address problems early enough

     B they eat badly

     C they don't exercise

29 An unexpected feature of his job is:

     A the regularity of his working week

     B the ability to choose his own hours

     C the contact with the public

30 In the long term he hopes to:

     A become financially independent

     B own his own practice

     C open his own chiropractic training school

Answer sheet: Cambridge B2 First Listening

Test No. ☐

Mark out of 30 ☐

Name _____   Date _____

Part 1: 8 marks

Mark the appropriate answer (A, B or C). | 0 | A ☐ B ▬ C ☐ |

1	A B C		5	A B C
2	A B C		6	A B C
3	A B C		7	A B C
4	A B C		8	A B C

Part 2: 10 marks

Write your answers in capital letters, using one box per letter.

| 0 | B | E | C | A | U | S | E | | | |

9.
10.
11.
12.
13.
14.
15.
16.
17.
18.

Answer sheet: Cambridge B2 First Listening

Part 3: 5 marks

Match the correct statement from the list (A-H).

0	Speaker 1	E

19	Speaker 1	
20	Speaker 2	
21	Speaker 3	
22	Speaker 4	
23	Speaker 5	

Part 4: 7 marks

Mark the appropriate answer (A, B or C).

0	A	**B**	C

24	A	B	C
25	A	B	C
26	A	B	C
27	A	B	C
28	A	B	C
29	A	B	C
30	A	B	C

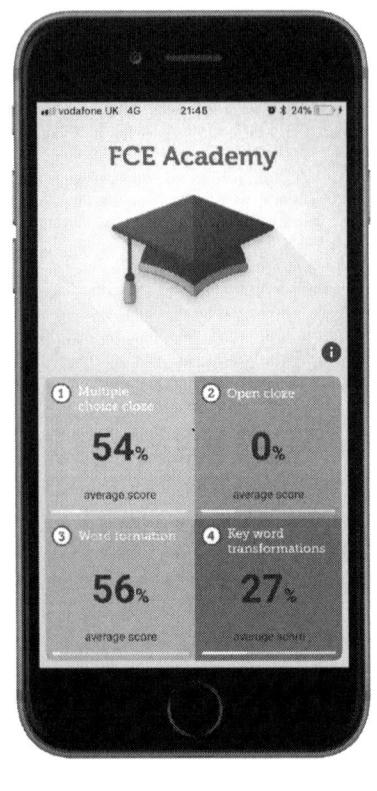

50% discount code: 050DAUQ0

Cambridge B2 First Listening

Test 2

Cambridge B2 First Listening

Part 1 — Test 2

Audio track: FCE_Listening_2_1.mp3

You will hear people speaking in eight different situations. For questions 1–8, select the best answer A, B, or C. Read the question carefully before playing the audio. In the exam, you will have the opportunity to listen to each recording twice.

1 You hear an urban-planning consultant talking about children's playgrounds in cities. What does she say about them?

    A Not enough importance is given to them by city councils

    B Safety standards have fallen

    C They only benefit children

2 You hear a man talking about being a teenager. What does he say about the experience?

    A He had a terrible time

    B He would never want to be a teenager again

    C It was a wonderful time

3 You hear two people talking about the local bus service. What do they say about it?

    A It's cheaper than the train

    B It's punctual

    C It's quick

4 You hear someone making an announcement about a TV schedule. What do they say?

    A The normal programme will be shown an hour later

    B This week's edition of 'Country Kitchen Time' will not be shown

    C 'Country Kitchen Time' will be shown on the internet instead

Cambridge B2 First Listening

Part 1   Cont.   Test 2

Audio track: FCE_Listening_2_1.mp3

5   You hear two pupils discussing their recent exam results. What do they agree on?

     A   The class should make a complaint about the teacher

     B   The exam contained material they had never seen before

     C   The exam was much more difficult than expected

6   You hear a PE teacher speaking. What does he say about Sports?

     A   The amount of sport played in schools should decrease

     B   Not everyone enjoys sport

     C   Sport is good for your mental abilities as well as your physical health

7   You hear a painter talking about a photography course she went on. What does she say about it?

     A   She didn't expect to enjoy it so much

     B   She has a new respect for photography

     C   It was a waste of time

8   You hear a women talking about having just run a marathon. How does she say she feels?

     A   Excited about the future

     B   Amazed by how much support she received

     C   Disappointed not to have won

Cambridge B2 First Listening

Part 2 — Test 2

Audio track: FCE_Listening_2_2.mp3

You will hear Mary Jones talking about a language course she went on. For questions 9–18, complete the sentence with a word or short phrase (a maximum of three words). Read the question carefully before playing the audio. In the exam, you will have the opportunity to listen to each recording twice.

She found out about the course from her [9] who was a former student on the course.

The course took place in [10] and lasted for three months. On the first day all the new students attended a welcome [11] in the language school.

Mary immediately made friends with Jill on the first day and they became [12]. Mary decided to have classes which took place in the [13] from Monday to Friday. For Mary [14] was the most difficult part of learning the new language. Surprisingly, Mary's favourite thing in Spain was the [15], which she enjoyed every day. She attended language exchanges at [16] and met people from all over the world.

Mary and Jill will keep in touch through Facebook and have promised to [17] every month.

Mary has now returned to the UK and has decided to study [18] at college.

Cambridge B2 First Listening

Part 3   Test 2

Audio track: Audio track: FCE_Listening_2_3.mp3

You will hear five different people talking about their relationships with animals. For questions 19–23, select from the list (A–H) what each person says. There are three extra statements which you do not have to use. Read the question carefully before playing the audio. In the exam, you will have the opportunity to listen to each recording twice.

Which person:

A   finds animals entertaining

B   has a problem with animals

C   earns money training animals

D   is terrified of a particular animal

E   works with a particular animal to do a vital job

F   has experience of working with animals in professional sport

G   does not believe animals should be domestic pets

H   admits to having an unrealistic image of an animal

Speaker 1		19
Speaker 2		20
Speaker 3		21
Speaker 4		22
Speaker 5		23

Cambridge B2 First Listening

Part 4   Test 2

Audio track: FCE_Listening_2_4.mp3

You will hear an interview with Colin Tracton, a sports scientist from Upton University. For questions 24–30, select the best answer A, B, or C. Read the question carefully before playing the audio. In the exam, you will have the opportunity to listen to each recording twice.

24   Colin first came to study at Upton University because:

         A   the location was convenient

         B   he was attracted by their Track and Field team

         C   he was offered a scholarship

25   His own sports career:

         A   was plagued by injury

         B   was long and distinguished

         C   was cut short because of a car crash

26   The theme of his final project during his degree was:

         A   an interesting new way to exercise

         B   nutrition

         C   allergies

27   He decided to continue studying:

         A   because he couldn't get a job

         B   after winning a prize

         C   after gaining exposure on a national TV show

Cambridge B2 First Listening

Part 4   Cont.   Test 2

Audio track: FCE_Listening_2_4.mp3

28   While giving advice to members of the public during a TV call-in, Colin remembers feeling:

       A   that he didn't have all the answers

       B   like a celebrity

       C   really shy.

29   High Intensity Interval Training is a type of exercise:

       A   that claims to get remarkable results in a much shorter time

       B   for lazy people

       C   that you need a trainer for

30   High Intensity Interval Training works by:

       A   tricking your body into feeling stressed

       B   targeting the core cardiovascular areas

       C   forcing you to sweat

Answer sheet: Cambridge B2 First Listening   Test No. ☐

Mark out of 30 ☐

Name _____   **Date** _____

Part 1:   8 marks

Mark the appropriate answer (A, B or C). | 0 | A B C |

1	A B C		5	A B C
2	A B C		6	A B C
3	A B C		7	A B C
4	A B C		8	A B C

Part 2:   10 marks

Write your answers in capital letters, using one box per letter.

| 0 | B | E | C | A | U | S | E | | | |

9																	
10																	
11																	
12																	
13																	
14																	
15																	
16																	
17																	
18																	

Answer sheet: Cambridge B2 First Listening

Part 3:   5 marks

Match the correct statement from the list (A-H).

| 0 | Speaker 1 | E |

19	Speaker 1	
20	Speaker 2	
21	Speaker 3	
22	Speaker 4	
23	Speaker 5	

Part 4:   7 marks

Mark the appropriate answer (A, B or C).

| 0 | A B C |

24	A B C
25	A B C
26	A B C
27	A B C
28	A B C
29	A B C
30	A B C

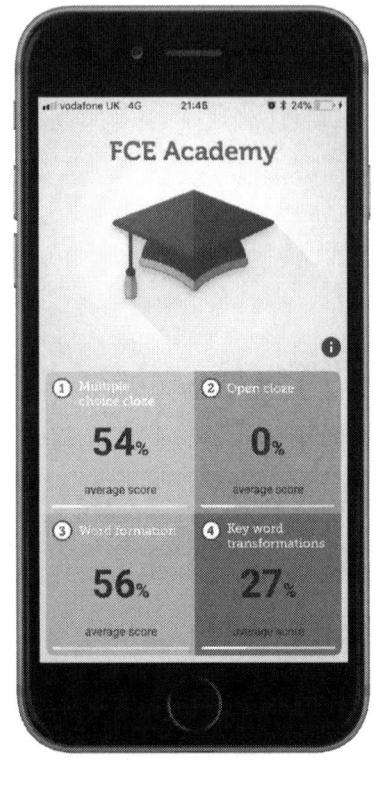

50% discount code: 050DAUQ0

24

Cambridge B2 First Listening

Test 3

Cambridge B2 First Listening

Part 1   Test 3

Audio track: FCE_Listening_3_1.mp3

You will hear people speaking in eight different situations. For questions 1–8, select the best answer A, B, or C. Read the question carefully before playing the audio. In the exam, you will have the opportunity to listen to each recording twice.

1. You hear someone speaking on the phone to a friend who has just failed her driving test. What is she doing?

    A   Offering to help her to learn

    B   Consoling her

    C   Explaining why her friend needs to try again

2. You hear a mother speaking with her daughter who is unable to come home for the weekend. How is the mother feeling?

    A   Resentful

    B   Happy to help

    C   Disappointed

3. You overhear two friends who have just watched a movie in the cinema. What do they agree was good about it?

    A   The special effects

    B   The main actor

    C   The script

4. You hear two people speaking about smartphones. What point does the woman make?

    A   Smartphones should not be allowed in schools

    B   A smartphone can be the most useful tool in modern living

    C   Smartphones are bad for your health

Cambridge B2 First Listening

Part 1   Cont.   Test 3

Audio track: FCE_Listening_3_1.mp3

5 You hear a teacher speaking to a student about their request to wear shorts in school. What is he saying?

    A He understands the student's point of view

    B He refuses to see the student's point of view

    C He thinks about reconsidering his position

6 You hear two students talking about preparing an essay. What are they both unsure about?

    A Which references to include

    B Including photos

    C Finishing before the deadline

7 You hear a tannoy announcement at a sports day. What is the speaker saying?

    A The Fun Run will take place earlier

    B The location of the food trucks will be changed

    C All runners should sign up on the internet

8 You hear a waiter speaking about his customers from the previous night. What does he say about them?

    A They were extremely famous

    B They didn't leave a tip

    C They were rude

Cambridge B2 First Listening

Part 2   Test 3

Audio track: FCE_Listening_3_2.mp3

You will hear Karen Smart talking about her job as a wildlife TV presenter. For questions 9–18, complete the sentence with a word or short phrase (a maximum of three words). Read the question carefully before playing the audio. In the exam, you will have the opportunity to listen to each recording twice.

When the camera crew first came to film her she was working as a [**9**]. Karen used a [**10**] to get the baby gorilla to trust her.

Karen went to [**11**] to work with mountain gorillas. Karen never returned to her original job because the TV show was a [**12**]. When Karen got back from being with the gorillas she was a [**13**].

Karen describes the 'orang pendek' as the [**14**] between apes and humans. In Sumatra they found a new kind of [**15**]. The lives of the British animals are described as just as [**16**] as their African counterparts.

Karen says human life would [**17**] if we were faced with the same problems animals are dealing with.

Karen feels [**18**] when she thinks of the incredible lives animals lead.

Cambridge B2 First Listening

Part 3   Test 3

Audio track: FCE_Listening_3_3.mp3

You will hear five different people talking about their summer holidays. For questions 19–23, select from the list (A–H) what each person speaks about. There are three extra statements which you do not have to use. Read the question carefully before playing the audio. In the exam, you will have the opportunity to listen to each recording twice.

Which person says:

A   they like watersport holidays

B   They don't want children around

C   backpacking is the only holiday for them

D   holidays are about new experiences

E   all-inclusive holidays are best for them

F   they go to the same resort every year

G   they love going on cruises

H   their holidays aren't very interesting

Speaker		Q
Speaker 1		19
Speaker 2		20
Speaker 3		21
Speaker 4		22
Speaker 5		23

Cambridge B2 First Listening

Part 4   Test 3

Audio track: FCE_Listening_3_4.mp3

You will hear an interview with a woman called Sally Jones, a traveller who has recently returned from Ethiopia. For questions 24–30, select the best answer A, B, or C. Read the question carefully before playing the audio. In the exam, you will have the opportunity to listen to each recording twice.

24 Why did Sally decide to travel to Ethiopia?

   A She hates going to places where there are large numbers of tourists

   B Vietnam was depressing

   C She wanted to see the countryside

25 When Sally visited Ethiopia, the country was:

   A dry and arid

   B in the middle of winter

   C lush and green.

26 Travellers within Ethiopia are recommended to:

   A avoid buses

   B travel only during the day

   C travel around the country

27 When arriving for the first time in Ethiopia, people are often surprised by:

   A the light

   B the green forests

   C the coffee

Cambridge B2 First Listening

Part 4   Cont.   Test 3

Audio track: FCE_Listening_3_4.mp3

28. Before going there the speaker didn't connect Ethiopia with:

    A   churches

    B   travel guides

    C   beautiful buildings

29. Sally says another surprising thing about Ethiopia is:

    A   only one other country in the world has an older Christian history

    B   the language doesn't have an alphabet

    C   time goes quickly there

30. In the last response Sally says Ethiopia is:

    A   not a friendly place

    B   building new houses

    C   developing its tourist industry

Answer sheet: Cambridge B2 First Listening

Test No. ☐

Mark out of 30 ☐

Name _____ **Date** _____

Part 1: 8 marks

Mark the appropriate answer (A, B or C). | 0 | A ☐ **B** ■ C ☐ |

1	A B C		5	A B C
2	A B C		6	A B C
3	A B C		7	A B C
4	A B C		8	A B C

Part 2: 10 marks

Write your answers in capital letters, using one box per letter.

| 0 | B | E | C | A | U | S | E | | | |

9.
10.
11.
12.
13.
14.
15.
16.
17.
18.

Answer sheet: Cambridge B2 First Listening

Part 3: 5 marks

Match the correct statement from the list (A-H).

| 0 | Speaker 1 | E |

19	Speaker 1	
20	Speaker 2	
21	Speaker 3	
22	Speaker 4	
23	Speaker 5	

Part 4: 7 marks

Mark the appropriate answer (A, B or C).

| 0 | A | **B** | C |

24	A	B	C
25	A	B	C
26	A	B	C
27	A	B	C
28	A	B	C
29	A	B	C
30	A	B	C

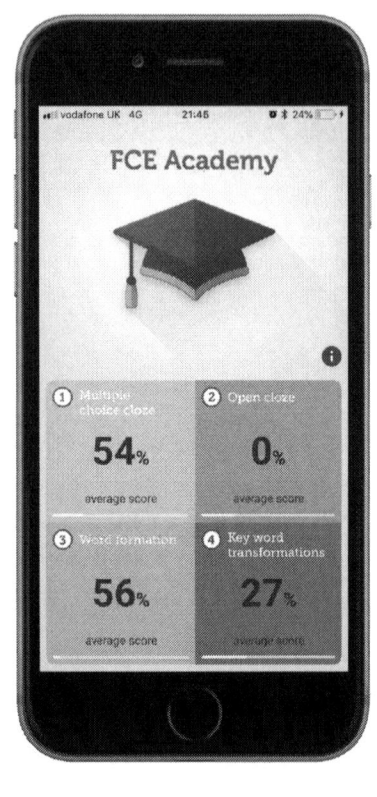

50% discount code: 050DAUQ0

Cambridge B2 First Listening

Test 4

Cambridge B2 First Listening

Part 1   Test 4

Audio track: FCE_Listening_4_1.mp3

You will hear people speaking in eight different situations. For questions 1–8, select the best answer A, B, or C. Read the question carefully before playing the audio. In the exam, you will have the opportunity to listen to each recording twice.

1   You hear two friends talking about a new computer. What does the man say about it?

    A   It's top of the range

    B   He needs it all the time

    C   It cost a lot more than he thought it would

2   You hear two friends discussing a play. What do they agree on?

    A   The acting was poor

    B   The scenery was incredible

    C   It was too long

3   You hear a man talking about his new job. What does he say?

    A   He is prepared to do whatever is necessary

    B   It will take a while to adjust

    C   The pay is very bad

4   You hear a woman comparing train travel and air travel. What does she say?

    A   She finds trains more convenient

    B   Traveling by train makes her stressed

    C   Air travel is the better option

Cambridge B2 First Listening

Part 1   Cont.   Test 4

Audio track: FCE_Listening_4_1.mp3

5   You hear a woman talking about the new restaurant on the high street. What did she enjoy?

       A   The spicy flavour

       B   The price

       C   The tea

6   You a hear a man talk about buying a new suit. What does he usually wear?

       A   Smart/casual clothing

       B   Formal suits

       C   Sportswear

7   You hear a woman asking for directions. What advice is she given?

       A   It's easier to walk

       B   Take a taxi

       C   Use a map

8   You hear a doctor giving advice over the phone to a patient. What instructions does he give?

       A   Go to bed and sleep

       B   Go straight to the hospital

       C   Make an appointment

Cambridge B2 First Listening

Part 2 — **Test 4**

Audio track: FCE_Listening_4_2.mp3

You will hear Caspian Ventura talk about his career as a freelance editor. For questions 9–18, complete the sentence with a word or short phrase (a maximum of three words). Read the question carefully before playing the audio. In the exam, you will have the opportunity to listen to each recording twice.

Caspian says [_____ 9 _____] your time is very important, as well as your accounts. It often takes 30 days before clients [_____ 10 _____] Caspian.

Caspian would [_____ 11 _____] someone who is thinking of becoming a freelance editor. Most correspondence occurs by [_____ 12 _____].

On more than one occasion Caspian has seen an author [_____ 13 _____] when they were given a copy of their book. Caspian's personal library is located in his [_____ 14 _____]. The strangest book he has ever worked on was about [_____ 15 _____].

Sometimes his friends get [_____ 16 _____] by his commenting on almost every subject.

It makes him [_____ 17 _____] if he reads something that contains too many errors due to bad editing.

His [_____ 18 _____] keeps him company while he works.

Cambridge B2 First Listening

Part 3   Test 4

Audio track: FCE_Listening_4_3.mp3

You will hear five different people talking about their boss. For questions 19–23, select from the list (A–H) what each person says. There are three extra statements which you do not have to use. Read the question carefully before playing the audio. In the exam, you will have the opportunity to listen to each recording twice.

Which person says:

A   they wouldn't do their boss' job

B   they think their boss needs to learn better management skills

C   they have always worked for the same boss

D   they have a conflict of interests

E   their boss often lies

F   they went on holiday with their boss

G   they went to school with their boss

H   they admire the work their boss does

Speaker 1		19
Speaker 2		20
Speaker 3		21
Speaker 4		22
Speaker 5		23

Cambridge B2 First Listening

Part 4   **Test 4**

Audio track: FCE_Listening_4_4.mp3

You will hear a radio interview with a street musician called Mike McShane. For questions 24–30, select the best answer A, B, or C. Read the question carefully before playing the audio. In the exam, you will have the opportunity to listen to each recording twice.

24   Buskers earn money from:

      A   donations from people

      B   ticket sales

      C   teaching

25   Mike got his licence for busking by:

      A   doing a type of test

      B   applying on the internet

      C   asking the police for permission

26   To be a busker:

      A   you need a licence

      B   you need to pass the audition

      C   there are no special requirements

27   What did Mike study at Music College?

      A   Guitar

      B   Piano

      C   Singing

Cambridge B2 First Listening

Part 4   **Cont.**   **Test 4**

Audio track: FCE_Listening_4_4.mp3

28 Mike became a busker because:

    A he was bored of being a teacher

    B he enjoys performing so much

    C of the financial stability

29 To play in the underground system you need to:

    A turn up from Friday–Sunday

    B write your name in a book

    C book your place on the internet

30 The negative aspect of playing with other buskers is:

    A They can be very unfriendly.

    B You have to share your earnings.

    C They can be unreliable.

Answer sheet: Cambridge B2 First Listening

Test No. ☐

Mark out of 30 ☐

Name _____ **Date** _____

Part 1: 8 marks

Mark the appropriate answer (A, B or C). | 0 | A B̲ C |

1	A B C		5	A B C
2	A B C		6	A B C
3	A B C		7	A B C
4	A B C		8	A B C

Part 2: 10 marks

Write your answers in capital letters, using one box per letter.

| 0 | B | E | C | A | U | S | E | | | |

9.
10.
11.
12.
13.
14.
15.
16.
17.
18.

Answer sheet: Cambridge B2 First Listening

Part 3:   5 marks

Match the correct statement from the list (A-H).

0	Speaker 1	E

19	Speaker 1	
20	Speaker 2	
21	Speaker 3	
22	Speaker 4	
23	Speaker 5	

Part 4:   7 marks

Mark the appropriate answer (A, B or C).

0	A	**B**	C

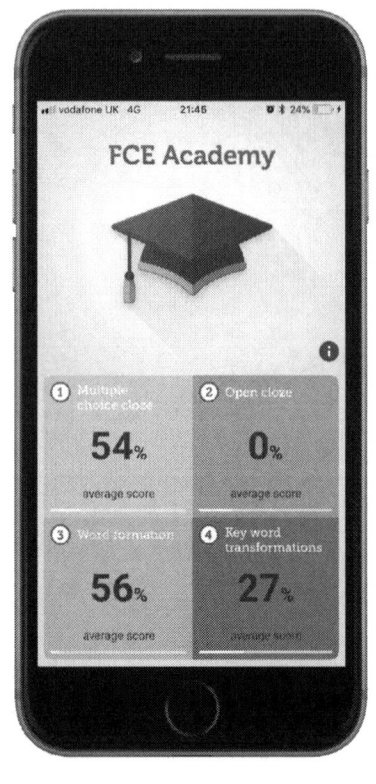

24	A	B	C
25	A	B	C
26	A	B	C
27	A	B	C
28	A	B	C
29	A	B	C
30	A	B	C

50% discount code: 050DAUQ0

PROSPERITY EDUCATION
www.prosperityeducation.net

Cambridge B2 First Listening

Test 5

Cambridge B2 First Listening

Part 1   Test 5

Audio track: FCE_Listening_5_1.mp3

You will hear people speaking in eight different situations. For questions 1–8, select the best answer A, B, or C. Read the question carefully before playing the audio. In the exam, you will have the opportunity to listen to each recording twice.

1. You hear two locals speak about tourists in their town. What do they agree on?

    A   They both hate tourists

    B   Tourists are good for the economy

    C   Tourists need to show more respect

2. You hear a professional soccer player talking about her last match. How does she feel?

    A   Angry at the referee

    B   Embarrassed about her performance

    C   Lucky to have won

3. You hear an announcement about public transport. What does it say?

    A   Maintenance work will affect services for two months

    B   Buses will replace all trains at the station

    C   A new line is being constructed

4. You hear a travel agent receiving a complaint from a customer over the phone. What was the problem?

    A   The entertainment at the resort

    B   The weather

    C   The pool wasn't open

Cambridge B2 First Listening

Part 1　　　　　　　　　　Cont.　　　　　　　　　　Test 5

Audio track: FCE_Listening_5_1.mp3

5 You hear an answering-machine message. What is the woman saying about the school pick-up today?

　A She would like to arrange a meeting with someone at the school

　B Someone else will come in her place

　C She will collect the kids from school as usual

6 You hear a street musician. Which music does he enjoy playing most?

　A Classical music

　B Pop music

　C Rock music

7 You hear someone speaking on the phone. What is wrong with the trousers?

　A They are too small

　B He doesn't like them

　C They have shrunk

8 You hear a weather forecast. What will the weather be like tomorrow?

　A Sunny

　B Wet

　C Icy

Cambridge B2 First Listening

Part 2   **Test 5**

Audio track: FCE_Listening_5_2.mp3

You will hear Sebastian, a children's summer camp director, talking about his job. For questions 9–18, complete the sentence with a word or short phrase (a maximum of three words). Read the question carefully before playing the audio. In the exam, you will have the opportunity to listen to each recording twice.

The children who attend the summer camp in July are [___ 9 ___] to the children who attend the school for the rest of the year. Sebastian's first job with Queen's College was as a [___ 10 ___]. Sebastian has worked for Queen's College for [___ 11 ___] years in total.

The most difficult part of his job is [___ 12 ___].

He says [___ 13 ___] is by far the most important aspect of his job.

Sebastian jokes that the task of transporting the children to the pool on buses requires [___ 14 ___].

Staff use badges and a [___ 15 ___] to check for children with food allergies.

Queen's College is very proud of its [___ 16 ___].

Last year one boy showed everyone his [___ 17 ___].

Everyone has a giant [___ 18 ___] after the Olympics on the last day.

Cambridge B2 First Listening

Part 3 — Test 5

Audio track: FCE_Listening_5_3.mp3

You will hear five different people talking about how they keep fit. For questions 19–23, select from the list (A–H) what each person says. There are three extra statements which you do not have to use. Read the question carefully before playing the audio. In the exam, you will have the opportunity to listen to each recording twice.

Which person:

A thinks exercising is old-fashioned

B finds the gym too expensive

C pays for the gym for the whole year

D thinks it is all just a passing trend

E doesn't feel they need to exercise

F has a rigid fitness routine

G thinks diet is the only consideration

H exercises best as part of a team

Speaker 1		19
Speaker 2		20
Speaker 3		21
Speaker 4		22
Speaker 5		23

Cambridge B2 First Listening

Part 4   Test 5

Audio track: FCE_Listening_5_4.mp3

You will hear an interview with John, a successful barrister, talking about his career. For questions 24–30, select the best answer A, B, or C. Read the question carefully before playing the audio. In the exam, you will have the opportunity to listen to each recording twice.

24   The main reason John became interested in Law was:

   A   his love of history

   B   his teacher

   C   the potential financial rewards

25   What were John's first impression of the Law?

   A   He was impressed by its content

   B   He was surprised by how difficult it was

   C   There was always a clear right or wrong answer

26   John says getting a good job depends on:

   A   your training

   B   the contacts you make

   C   being the brightest candidate

27   John recommends getting to know legal companies by:

   A   looking on the internet

   B   going to the company's building

   C   Travelling a great deal.

Cambridge B2 First Listening

Part 4   Cont.   Test 5

Audio track: FCE_Listening_5_4.mp3

28   John says the ideal way of resolving disputes is:

      A   by coming to an agreement without going to court

      B   in court

      C   by him doing his job properly

29   Which negative aspect of his work does John speak about?

      A   The travelling

      B   Attending conferences

      C   The long working hours

30   What does John enjoy most about his job now?

      A   The pay

      B   The variety

      C   Meeting people

Answer sheet: Cambridge B2 First Listening   Test No. ☐

Mark out of 30 ☐

Name _____   **Date** _____

Part 1:   8 marks

Mark the appropriate answer (A, B or C). | 0 | A ☐ B ▬ C ☐ |

1	A B C		5	A B C
2	A B C		6	A B C
3	A B C		7	A B C
4	A B C		8	A B C

Part 2:   10 marks

Write your answers in capital letters, using one box per letter.

| 0 | B | E | C | A | U | S | E | | | |

| 9 |
| 10 |
| 11 |
| 12 |
| 13 |
| 14 |
| 15 |
| 16 |
| 17 |
| 18 |

Answer sheet: Cambridge B2 First Listening

Part 3:   5 marks

Match the correct statement from the list (A-H).

0	Speaker 1	E

19	Speaker 1	
20	Speaker 2	
21	Speaker 3	
22	Speaker 4	
23	Speaker 5	

Part 4:   7 marks

Mark the appropriate answer (A, B or C).

0	A	**B**	C	

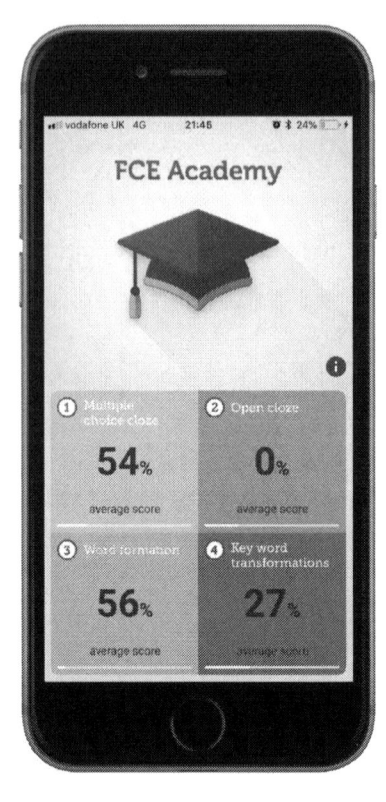

24	A	B	C	
25	A	B	C	
26	A	B	C	
27	A	B	C	
28	A	B	C	
29	A	B	C	
30	A	B	C	

50% discount code: 050DAUQ0

PROSPERITY EDUCATION
www.prosperityeducation.net

Cambridge B2 First Listening

Test 6

Cambridge B2 First Listening

Part 1 — Test 6

Audio track: FCE_Listening_6_1.mp3

You will hear people speaking in eight different situations. For questions 1–8, select the best answer A, B, or C. Read the question carefully before playing the audio. In the exam, you will have the opportunity to listen to each recording twice.

1. You hear two customers talking in a hairdressing salon. What style does one recommend?

    A   Short

    B   Long

    C   Curly

2. You hear a woman talking about the time her son forgot her birthday. What does she say he did to apologise?

    A   He visited her

    B   He sent flowers

    C   He arranged a video call

3. You hear a mechanic talking to a customer. What's the problem with the car?

    A   The tyres need to be changed

    B   The car is very old

    C   The engine has a problem

4. You hear a nurse talking. Why did she become a nurse?

    A   Her mother was a doctor

    B   She needed a job

    C   She wanted to work with children

Cambridge B2 First Listening

Part 1 **Cont.** **Test 6**

Audio track: FCE_Listening_6_1.mp3

5 You hear a bus driver speaking about his job. What's the worst part of the job for him?

   A Working alone

   B The pay

   C Working irregular hours

6 You hear two historians speaking. What are they talking about?

   A Ancient Egypt

   B Prehistoric Man

   C Roman culture

7 You hear Tom talking about his boss, Rich. What does he say about him?

   A Rich's reactions are difficult to predict

   B Rich often has bad days

   C Rich's mood affects how he works

8 You hear a woman talking about her wedding. Where is the wedding going to take place?

   A In a traditional setting

   B In an exotic location

   C Somewhere unexpected

Cambridge B2 First Listening

Part 2   Test 6

Audio track: FCE_Listening_6_2.mp3

You will hear Rob Baxendale talking about learning to play the cello at the age of 40. For questions 9–18, complete the sentence with a word or short phrase (a maximum of three words). Read the question carefully before playing the audio. In the exam, you will have the opportunity to listen to each recording twice.

Rob says that when people start working and having families they often lose their [_____ 9 _____] for the interests they had as youngsters. He felt inspired to start playing again after watching his [_____ 10 _____] play. Rob's daughter has helped him to [_____ 11 _____] many of the simple tunes he used to know. Learning as an adult, he appreciates how important [_____ 12 _____] is to your playing.

Rob's teacher has recently relocated from [_____ 13 _____].

Rob is able to do around [_____ 14 _____] of homework a week.

It takes [_____ 15 _____] hours of practice to become an expert in something. Rob calculated it would take him [_____ 16 _____] years to become an expert at the rate he practises. Rob has most problems with [_____ 17 _____].

He says learning to [_____ 18 _____] the cello is the most important thing.

Cambridge B2 First Listening

Part 3   Test 6

Audio track: FCE_Listening_6_3.mp3

You will hear five different people talking about teachers from their school days. For questions 19–23, select from the list (A–H) what each person says. There are three extra statements which you do not have to use. Read the question carefully before playing the audio. In the exam, you will have the opportunity to listen to each recording twice.

Which person says their teacher:

A   was really cruel to them

Speaker 1		19

B   showed how the skills could be useful in real life

Speaker 2		20

C   taught negative stereotypes

Speaker 3		21

D   taught positive values

Speaker 4		22

E   Was someone they looked up to

Speaker 5		23

F   ignored them

G   was like a parental figure

H   made them feel embarrassed

Cambridge B2 First Listening

Part 4   **Test 6**

Audio track: FCE_Listening_6_4.mp3

You will hear an interview with a woman called Sarah Mortimer, a body painter. For questions 24–30, select the best answer A, B, or C. Read the question carefully before playing the audio. In the exam, you will have the opportunity to listen to each recording twice.

24   Sarah says she first took up face painting:

        A   at school

        B   while at Art College

        C   after watching a documentary on the subject

25   The reason Sarah was particularly interested in face painting during her college years was:

        A   the reactions from the people she painted

        B   the financial benefit

        C   she could make other people better-looking

26   Sarah started taking body painting seriously when:

        A   she read an article

        B   she built a website

        C   her husband became a clown

27   Sarah got some top-class tuition in body painting as a result of:

        A   knowing some influential people

        B   her university studies

        C   winning a competition

Cambridge B2 First Listening

Part 4   Cont.   Test 6

Audio track: FCE_Listening_6_4.mp3

28 What impressed the teacher of the masterclass?

    A Sarah´s professionalism

    B Sarah´s problem-solving skills

    C Sarah´s artistic skills

29 Why did Sarah decide to become an Art Therapist?

    A To help other people

    B To become a doctor

    C To make more money

30 Sarah says the world of body painting opened up to here when:

    A she won a prize

    B she attended a masterclass

    C she realised how similar it was to tattooing.

Answer sheet: Cambridge B2 First Listening   Test No. [ ]

Mark out of 30 [ ]

Name _____   Date _____

Part 1:   8 marks

Mark the appropriate answer (A, B or C).   0 A [B] C

1	A B C		5	A B C
2	A B C		6	A B C
3	A B C		7	A B C
4	A B C		8	A B C

Part 2:   10 marks

Write your answers in capital letters, using one box per letter.

0 | B | E | C | A | U | S | E | | | |

9
10
11
12
13
14
15
16
17
18

Answer sheet: Cambridge B2 First Listening

Part 3: 5 marks

Match the correct statement from the list (A-H).

| 0 | Speaker 1 | E |

19	Speaker 1	
20	Speaker 2	
21	Speaker 3	
22	Speaker 4	
23	Speaker 5	

Part 4: 7 marks

Mark the appropriate answer (A, B or C).

| 0 | A | **B** | C |

24	A	B	C
25	A	B	C
26	A	B	C
27	A	B	C
28	A	B	C
29	A	B	C
30	A	B	C

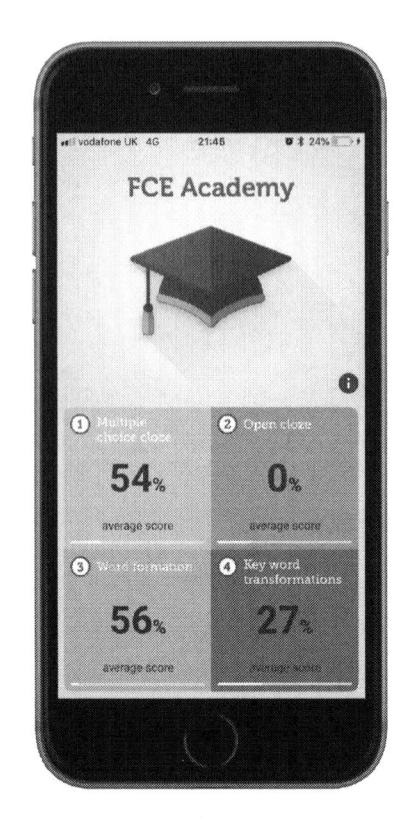

50% discount code: 050DAUQ0

Cambridge B2 First Listening

Test 7

Cambridge B2 First Listening

Part 1   Test 7

Audio track: FCE_Listening_7_1.mp3

You will hear people speaking in eight different situations. For questions 1–8, select the best answer A, B, or C. Read the question carefully before playing the audio. In the exam, you will have the opportunity to listen to each recording twice.

1   You hear two writers speaking about a piece of work. How do they feel?

    A   Disappointed

    B   Satisfied

    C   Anxious

2   You hear a swimmer talking about her career. What does she think she would like to do next?

    A   Nothing connected with sports

    B   Work in the media

    C   Train for another competition

3   You hear a man calling his gym about a class. Why is he calling?

    A   To make an appointment

    B   To get more information

    C   To make a complaint

4   You hear two friends speaking about an app. What do they agree on?

    A   It's useful

    B   It's interesting

    C   It's easy to use

Cambridge B2 First Listening

Part 1   **Cont.**   **Test 7**

Audio track: FCE_Listening_7_1.mp3

5 You hear a man talking about his job. How does he feel?

     A Enthusiastic

     B Confused

     C Bored

6 You hear a woman talking on the phone about an order she has made. What does she say?

     A The items will arrive today

     B The order needs to be cancelled

     C The items can be delivered tomorrow

7 You hear a taxi driver talking to a passenger. What can't the passenger do?

     A Pick someone up

     B Pay using a credit card

     C Remember where to go

8 You hear two people talking in a supermarket. What do they agree on?

     A It's too expensive

     B The supermarket closes too early

     C There is a good range of products

Cambridge B2 First Listening

Part 2 — **Test 7**

Audio track: FCE_Listening_7_2.mp3

You will hear Duncan, a keen surfer from Sydney in Australia. For questions 9–18, complete the sentence with a word or short phrase (a maximum of three words). Read the question carefully before playing the audio. In the exam, you will have the opportunity to listen to each recording twice.

Duncan is happy to fulfil the [___9___] of an Australian surfer.

He prefers Manly Beach because it's not as [___10___] as the more famous Bondi Beach.

On a Saturday Duncan travels by [___11___] to get to Manly Beach.

Duncan would not recommend the north end of the beach for [___12___] surfers.

Everyone should know that [___13___] is given to the first surfer to reach a wave. Abandoned surf boards can [___14___] other surfers.

A 'rip tide' is described as a [___15___] that heads out to sea. Duncan recommends being [___16___] before starting surfing.

Duncan uses [___17___] to help remove old wax from his board. The wax needed for surfboards in Australia is [___18___] to the wax needed for surfing in Europe.

Cambridge B2 First Listening

Part 3   Test 7

Audio track: FCE_Listening_7_3.mp3

You will hear five different people talking about their experience of working at a holiday resort. For questions 19–23, select from the list (A–H) the reason each person gives for doing their hobby. There are three extra statements which you do not have to use. Read the question carefully before playing the audio. In the exam, you will have the opportunity to listen to each recording twice.

Which person says:

A   they don't enjoy the work at all

B   they love the variety of the job

C   they wouldn't recommend it to anyone

D   they will not be working for the company again

E   the pay is really good

F   it's a dream come true

G   they met a partner there

H   It's a great step on the career ladder

Speaker 1		19
Speaker 2		20
Speaker 3		21
Speaker 4		22
Speaker 5		23

Cambridge B2 First Listening

Part 4   **Test 7**

Audio track: FCE_Listening_7_4.mp3

You will hear an interview with Dave Willis, a teacher at an international school in Malaysia. For questions 24–30, select the best answer A, B, or C. Read the question carefully before playing the audio. In the exam, you will have the opportunity to listen to each recording twice.

24 Dave became unhappy teaching in the UK because:

    A of the large amount of paperwork required

    B of all the planning needed

    C he was not benefiting the children

25 Fewer teachers would leave the system if:

    A the pay was better

    B policymakers listened to teachers' advice

    C they weren't idealists

26 When moving to Spain, Dave had problems with:

    A the distance between the UK and Spain

    B the administration

    C leaving so many friends and family behind

27 In Dave's experience, parents of children in international schools:

    A have high expectations that their children will do well

    B are happier than they were in the UK

    C complain more than British parents do

Cambridge B2 First Listening

Part 4   Cont.   Test 7

Audio track: FCE_Listening_7_4.mp3

28 In the classroom, more modern schools want students to:

    A do homework

    B listen

    C participate

29 At the end of the interview, what is Dave unsure about doing in Malaysia?

    A settling

    B sending his kids to school

    C retiring

30 When does Dave think he'll have to decide on his future?

    A immediately

    B when he gets a bit older

    C when his children finish school

Answer sheet: Cambridge B2 First Listening

Test No. ☐

Mark out of 30 ☐

Name _____ **Date** _____

Part 1: 8 marks

Mark the appropriate answer (A, B or C). | 0 | A ☐ B ▄ C ☐ |

1	A B C		5	A B C
2	A B C		6	A B C
3	A B C		7	A B C
4	A B C		8	A B C

Part 2: 10 marks

Write your answers in capital letters, using one box per letter.

| 0 | B | E | C | A | U | S | E | | | |

9																		
10																		
11																		
12																		
13																		
14																		
15																		
16																		
17																		
18																		

Answer sheet: Cambridge B2 First Listening

Part 3: 5 marks

Match the correct statement from the list (A-H).

0	Speaker 1	E

19	Speaker 1	
20	Speaker 2	
21	Speaker 3	
22	Speaker 4	
23	Speaker 5	

Part 4: 7 marks

Mark the appropriate answer (A, B or C).

0	A	**B**	C

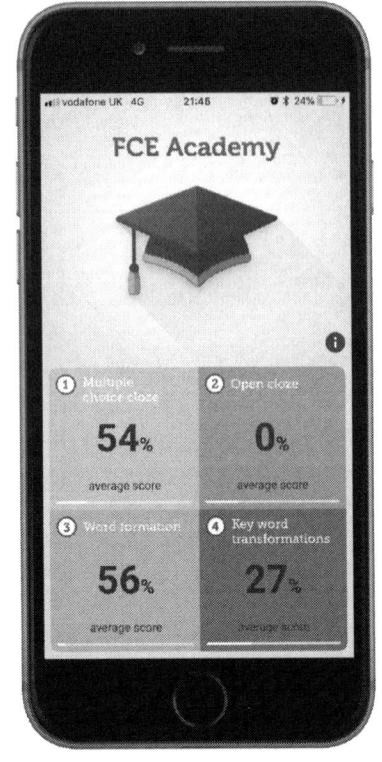

24	A	B	C
25	A	B	C
26	A	B	C
27	A	B	C
28	A	B	C
29	A	B	C
30	A	B	C

50% discount code: O5ODAUQO

Cambridge B2 First Listening

Test 8

Cambridge B2 First Listening

Part 1   Test 8

Audio track: FCE_Listening_8_1.mp3

You will hear people speaking in eight different situations. For questions 1–8, select the best answer A, B, or C. Read the question carefully before playing the audio. In the exam, you will have the opportunity to listen to each recording twice.

1   You hear a woman talking about her weekend. What did she do?

   A   She had a party
   B   She went camping
   C   She played sports

2   You hear a man describing yesterday's meeting. How did his boss behave?

   A   unusually
   B   helpfully
   C   aggressively

3   You hear two people discussing the weather. How is the weather going to be tomorrow, according to the forecast?

   A   Raining
   B   Freezing
   C   Sunny

4   You hear two students talking. What is the problem?

   A   The bus did not come
   B   The train was late
   C   They took the wrong route

Cambridge B2 First Listening

Part 1　　　　　　　　　Cont.　　　　　　　　　Test 8

Audio track: FCE_Listening_8_1.mp3

5　You hear two people talking about the music they are listening to. What does the woman say about the music playing?

　　A　It always cheers her up
　　B　It always makes her sad
　　C　It reminds her of someone

6　You hear a woman talking about a crime series on TV. What does she say about the storylines?

　　A　They are not believable
　　B　They are really varied and different every week
　　C　They are predictable

7　Two men are talking about a class at the gym. What objective do they both have?

　　A　To get to know the teacher
　　B　To get fit
　　C　To win a competition

8　You hear a doctor talk to a patient about their injury. What does the doctor advise them to do?

　　A　Keep working out
　　B　Stop exercising immediately
　　C　Try a different type of exercise

Cambridge B2 First Listening

Part 2 — Test 8

Audio track: FCE_Listening_8_2.mp3

You will hear Jerome Lightyear talking about his career as a commercial airline pilot. For questions 9–18, complete the sentence with a word or short phrase (a maximum of three words). Read the question carefully before playing the audio. In the exam, you will have the opportunity to listen to each recording twice.

You can get your qualification in 18 months if you do it [9].

Jerome did [10] so didn't need to pay for his own training.

Jerome says having a [11] is not necessary to become a pilot.

You need to fly for at least [12] hours before becoming a captain.

Jerome has been a pilot for [13].

He describes pilots as [14].

Jerome says pilots often feel [15] after work.

Jerome loves the idea that every flight will be [16].

He says [17] so much can put a strain on his relationships.

Jerome's wife is described as [18].

Cambridge B2 First Listening

Part 3   Test 8

Audio track: FCE_Listening_8_3.mp3

You will hear five different people talking about their hobbies and interests. For questions 19–23, select from the list (A–H) the reason each person gives for doing their hobby. There are three extra statements which you do not have to use. Read the question carefully before playing the audio. In the exam, you will have the opportunity to listen to each recording twice.

Which person says they do their hobby to:

A   annoy someone

B   earn money

C   keep fit

D   learn

E   meet people

F   forget about work

G   impress people

H   deal with stress

Speaker 1		19

Speaker 2		20

Speaker 3		21

Speaker 4		22

Speaker 5		23

Cambridge B2 First Listening

Part 4   Test 8

Audio track: FCE_Listening_8_4.mp3

You will hear an interview with Ray Portman, who has written a book called *Walking El Camino*. For questions 24–30, select the best answer A, B, or C. Read the question carefully before playing the audio. In the exam, you will have the opportunity to listen to each recording twice.

24   What could Ray do during his walk that brought a profound change to his life?

     A   Walk

     B   Think

     C   Be alone

25   What happened to cause Ray to look for a change in his life?

     A   An important relationship ended

     B   A job changed

     C   He had a spiritual awakening

26   Walkers can start their journeys from:

     A   France

     B   anywhere

     C   Spain

27   How does Ray describe the accommodation?

     A   Old

     B   Interesting

     C   Basic

Cambridge B2 First Listening

Part 4   Cont.   Test 8

Audio track: FCE_Listening_8_4.mp3

28. What does Ray admit to doing upon arriving in Santiago de Compostela?

     A   Quitting

     B   Crying

     C   Sleeping

29. What advice does Ray give to anyone thinking about walking the *Camino*?

     A   Buy good shoes

     B   Don't do it

     C   Complete it

30. What comment does Ray make about the Camino walkers?

     A   They are mostly teenagers?

     B   They are mostly older people.

     C   They come from all parts of society.

Answer sheet: Cambridge B2 First Listening   Test No. ☐

Mark out of 30 ☐

Name _____   **Date** _____

Part 1:   8 marks

Mark the appropriate answer (A, B or C). | 0 | A ☐ B ■ C ☐ |

1	A ☐ B ☐ C ☐		5	A ☐ B ☐ C ☐
2	A ☐ B ☐ C ☐		6	A ☐ B ☐ C ☐
3	A ☐ B ☐ C ☐		7	A ☐ B ☐ C ☐
4	A ☐ B ☐ C ☐		8	A ☐ B ☐ C ☐

Part 2:   10 marks

Write your answers in capital letters, using one box per letter.

| 0 | B | E | C | A | U | S | E | | | |

9.
10.
11.
12.
13.
14.
15.
16.
17.
18.

Answer sheet: Cambridge B2 First Listening

Part 3:   5 marks

Match the correct statement from the list (A-H).

0	Speaker 1	E

19	Speaker 1	
20	Speaker 2	
21	Speaker 3	
22	Speaker 4	
23	Speaker 5	

Part 4:   7 marks

Mark the appropriate answer (A, B or C).

0	A	**B**	C

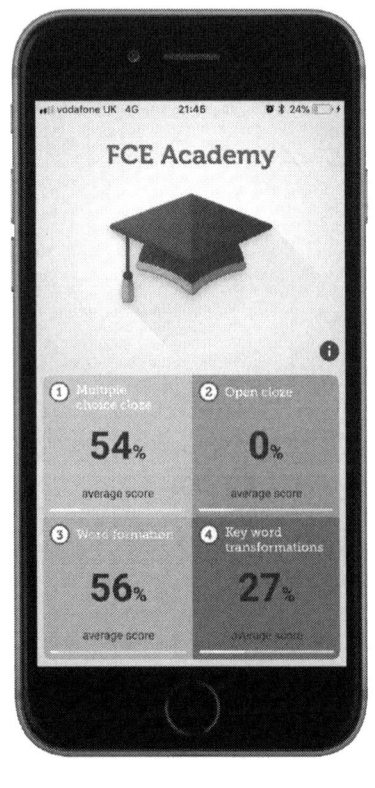

24	A	B	C
25	A	B	C
26	A	B	C
27	A	B	C
28	A	B	C
29	A	B	C
30	A	B	C

50% discount code: 050DAUQ0

PROSPERITY EDUCATION
www.prosperityeducation.net

Cambridge B2 First Listening

Test 9

Cambridge B2 First Listening

Part 1   Test 9

Audio track: FCE_Listening_9_1.mp3

You will hear people speaking in eight different situations. For questions 1–8, select the best answer A, B, or C. Read the question carefully before playing the audio. In the exam, you will have the opportunity to listen to each recording twice.

1   You hear a careers consultant describing a teacher's job to some students. What drawback does she warn of?

   A   Negative health effects
   B   Lots of planning time
   C   Lots of unpaid work

2   You hear a man talking about a place he used to visit as a child. What point is he making?

   A   Children need to be taken on fancy holidays nowadays
   B   Children are happy as long as they are having fun
   C   Holidays are not as good as they used to be

3   You hear a police officer taking details of an incident from a member of the public. What crime is being reported?

   A   Stealing
   B   Someone is making excessive noise
   C   An assault

4   You hear a kitchen salesman speaking with a customer. Why is his shop better than the competition?

   A   the customer service
   B   the larger range available
   C   the quality of its products

Cambridge B2 First Listening

Part 1   **Cont.**   **Test 9**

Audio track: FCE_Listening_9_1.mp3

5 You hear a man speaking with his friend on the phone. Why won't he be going on the trip with his friend?

    A He can't pay for it

    B He doesn't think it's good value for money

    C He can't get the time away from work

6 You hear two women arranging a journey. What do they agree on?

    A Who is going to drive

    B What time to return home

    C How long it will take to get there

7 You hear a woman asking for advice from a pharmacist. What does the pharmacist say the women must do?

    A Have surgery immediately

    B Try another pharmacy

    C Get a prescription from a doctor

8 You hear a physicist talking about playing the violin. What does he say about it?

    A He sees similarities between science and music

    B It helps him solve problems

    C He thinks it is more difficult than Physics

Cambridge B2 First Listening

Part 2
Test 9
Audio track: FCE_Listening_9_2.mp3

You will hear Paul Oswald talking about his hobby, wild swimming. For questions 9–18, complete the sentence with a word or short phrase (a maximum of three words). Read the question carefully before playing the audio. In the exam, you will have the opportunity to listen to each recording twice.

Wild swimming is described as swimming in [9] water.

Paul decided to get involved with an outdoor activity when he realised he never saw [10].

Paul's first wild swim lasted no more than [11].

Paul's favourite place to swim is from a river [12].

He likes to [13] on a rock on an island.

In the beginning Paul worried about [14].

Paul advises new wild swimmers to build up [15].

Paul says [16] is the biggest problem that wild swimmers face. Access is important and Paul says always choose a place with convenient [17] close to where you will swim.

Paul says having a good [18] to look forward to motivates him when he is swimming.

Cambridge B2 First Listening

Part 3
Test 9
Audio track: FCE_Listening_9_3.mp3

You will hear five different people talking about buying a home. For questions 19–23, select from the list (A–H) what each person says. There are three extra statements which you do not have to use. Read the question carefully before playing the audio. In the exam, you will have the opportunity to listen to each recording twice.

Which person says:

A   they let the agent do all the hard work

B   it's the most stressful thing they have ever experienced

C   they know how to save lots of money

D   they move home frequently

E   they only get involved after the house has been purchased

F   they love the viewing process

G   they will never move house again

H   it's a simple process

Speaker 1		19
Speaker 2		20
Speaker 3		21
Speaker 4		22
Speaker 5		23

Cambridge B2 First Listening

Part 4 — Test 9

Audio track: FCE_Listening_9_4.mp3

You will hear an interview with Annie Williams, who has always dreamed of being a writer. For questions 24–30, select the best answer A, B, or C. Read the question carefully before playing the audio. In the exam, you will have the opportunity to listen to each recording twice.

24 Annie says that when she was young, like most aspiring writers, she was a:

   A fan

   B good student

   C movie-goer

25 Where does Annie recommend looking for interesting, unknown writers?

   A At conventions

   B On the internet

   C In book shops

26 Annie thinks some of the unknown writers' work is:

   A better than her work

   B worse than her work

   C of a similar quality to her work.

27 Annie thinks she became successful because:

   A she was lucky

   B she got to know influential people

   C she wrote a blog

Cambridge B2 First Listening

Part 4　　　　　　　　　　　Cont.　　　　　　　　　　　Test 9

Audio track: FCE_Listening_9_4.mp3

28　What is Annie's main point of contact with her fans?

　　A　Conventions

　　B　Her website

　　C　Her books

29　Annie thinks fantasy books are:

　　A　more popular with women

　　B　more popular with men

　　C　equally popular with men and women

30　For Annie, the purpose of the interview is to:

　　A　promote her latest book

　　B　speak about the writing process

　　C　talk about her website

Answer sheet: Cambridge B2 First Listening   Test No. ☐

Mark out of 30 ☐

Name _____   **Date** _____

Part 1:   8 marks

Mark the appropriate answer (A, B or C). | 0 | A B̲ C |

1	A B C		5	A B C
2	A B C		6	A B C
3	A B C		7	A B C
4	A B C		8	A B C

Part 2:   10 marks

Write your answers in capital letters, using one box per letter.

| 0 | B | E | C | A | U | S | E | | | |

9. _____
10. _____
11. _____
12. _____
13. _____
14. _____
15. _____
16. _____
17. _____
18. _____

Answer sheet: Cambridge B2 First Listening

Part 3:   5 marks

Match the correct statement from the list (A-H).

0	Speaker 1	E

19	Speaker 1	
20	Speaker 2	
21	Speaker 3	
22	Speaker 4	
23	Speaker 5	

Part 4:   7 marks

Mark the appropriate answer (A, B or C).

0	A	**B**	C

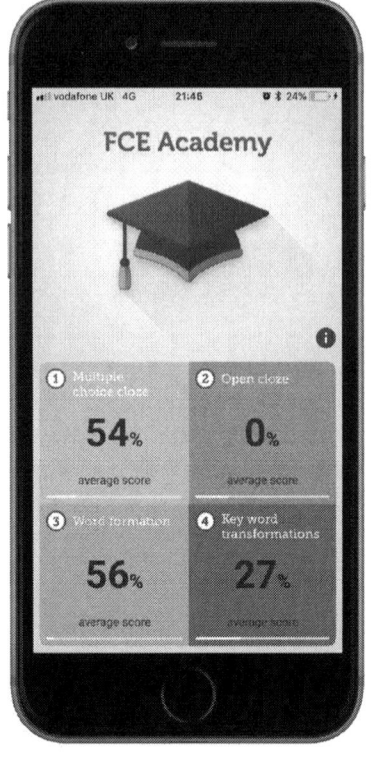

24	A	B	C
25	A	B	C
26	A	B	C
27	A	B	C
28	A	B	C
29	A	B	C
30	A	B	C

Cambridge B2 First Listening

Test 10

Cambridge B2 First Listening

Part 1   Test 10

Audio track: FCE_Listening_10_1.mp3

You will hear people speaking in eight different situations. For questions 1–8, select the best answer A, B, or C. Read the question carefully before playing the audio. In the exam, you will have the opportunity to listen to each recording twice.

1   You hear a woman talking on the phone about a missing item from the shopping she has ordered online. How does she feel?

    A   Sympathetic to the supermarket's situation

    B   Annoyed by the attitude of the supermarket staff

    C   Disappointed about the service provided

2   You overhear two friends speaking about a movie they have just seen. What do they agree on?

    A   The leading actor's obvious talent

    B   The need for the story to be believable

    C   Their reasons for going to the cinema

3   You hear a worker talking about his job. What does he say about it?

    A   It's enjoyable

    B   It's difficult

    C   It's boring

4   You hear a woman talking about gaining a place on a university course. What is she doing?

    A   Admitting excitement about commencing her studies

    B   Explaining why she thinks she was chosen

    C   Expressing surprise about being accepted

Cambridge B2 First Listening

Part 1   Cont.   Test 10

Audio track: FCE_Listening_10_1.mp3

5. You hear a businessman calling a businesswoman. What do they discuss?

     A   how long she needs to stay

     B   the time constraints of their next meeting

     C   changing plans

6. You hear a woman speaking to a sales assistant in a shop. Why can't she have a refund?

     A   It is outside the time period in which refunds are given

     B   She is not in the right place

     C   Something is wrong with the item

7. You hear a man making a statement. Who is talking?

     A   A journalist

     B   A teacher

     C   A member of the police

8. You hear a conversation between a salesperson and a customer. What is being bought?

     A   A car

     B   A washing machine

     C   An instrument

Cambridge B2 First Listening

Part 2 **Test 10**

Audio track: FCE_Listening_10_2.mp3

You will hear Steve Barlow talking about his career as a professional pianist. For questions 9–18, complete the sentence with a word or short phrase (a maximum of three words). Read the question carefully before playing the audio. In the exam, you will have the opportunity to listen to each recording twice.

Steve's first musical experience was playing [____9____] although his main instrument is now the violin. Steve is open to the idea of [____10____], but does not have to do it to earn money. The most important characteristic showed by his teachers when helping him achieve success was [____11____].

Steve warns aspiring musicians against neglecting important skills, such as [____12____].

Playing [____13____] will help with this, as it will when composing and when in the classroom. Taking part in paid or unpaid activities is essential to [____14____].

Remembering that being a [____15____] is really Important too. Musicians must keep [____16____] to deal with the physical requirements of being a musician. Performing musicians must be aware of how the public sees them, and Steve points out the importance of [____17____] For this.

In recent times those who have been the most successful have also been the best at [____18____].

Cambridge B2 First Listening

Part 3   Test 10

Audio track: FCE_Listening_10_3.mp3

You will hear five different people talking about their experience of job interviews. For questions 19–23, select from the list (A–H) what each person says. There are three extra statements which you do not have to use. Read the question carefully before playing the audio. In the exam, you will have the opportunity to listen to each recording twice.

Which person says:

A   try to find out about the interviewer's personal life

| Speaker 1 | | 19 |

B   compromise on your principles

| Speaker 2 | | 20 |

C   flexibility makes you more employable

| Speaker 3 | | 21 |

D   wear very fashionable clothes

| Speaker 4 | | 22 |

E   dress in an appropriate way

| Speaker 5 | | 23 |

F   be open and honest

G   be considerate as well as punctual

H   investigate your prospective employer to gain knowledge and confidence

Cambridge B2 First Listening

Part 4   Test 10

Audio track: FCE_Listening_10_4.mp3

You will hear an interview with Charlotte Orwell, who has a peculiar hobby. For questions 24–30, select the best answer A, B, or C. Read the question carefully before playing the audio. In the exam, you will have the opportunity to listen to each recording twice.

24 Charlotte's first non-fiction piece of writing looked behind the scenes at which places in London?

   A Post offices
   B Museums
   C Offices

25 Charlotte was particularly interested in the stamp collectors':

   A tools
   B hobbies
   C vocabulary

26 What function does Charlotte say the share certificates perform?

   A They provide a historical record of society
   B They reveal who had a lot of money
   C They tell us which companies were successful

27 Which types of postcards are the most valuable?

   A The rudest ones
   B The most unusual ones
   C The oldest ones

Cambridge B2 First Listening

Part 4   Cont.   Test 10

Audio track: FCE_Listening_10_4.mp3

28   Charlotte says the items which people collect almost always:

     A   cost the collector more than they will earn

     B   earn the collector more than they cost

     C   are of no value at all.

29   The largest sums of money in the world of collecting are spent on:

     A   cars

     B   art

     C   stamps

30   Charlotte's next book will be about:

     A   carpets

     B   watches

     C   Space

Answer sheet: Cambridge B2 First Listening   Test No. ☐

Mark out of 30 ☐

Name _____   Date _____

Part 1:   8 marks

Mark the appropriate answer (A, B or C). | 0 | A ☐ B ■ C ☐ |

1	A B C		5	A B C
2	A B C		6	A B C
3	A B C		7	A B C
4	A B C		8	A B C

Part 2:   10 marks

Write your answers in capital letters, using one box per letter.

| 0 | B | E | C | A | U | S | E | | | |

9.
10.
11.
12.
13.
14.
15.
16.
17.
18.

Answer sheet: Cambridge B2 First Listening

Part 3: 5 marks

Match the correct statement from the list (A-H).

0	Speaker 1	E

19	Speaker 1	
20	Speaker 2	
21	Speaker 3	
22	Speaker 4	
23	Speaker 5	

Part 4: 7 marks

Mark the appropriate answer (A, B or C).

0	A	**B**	C

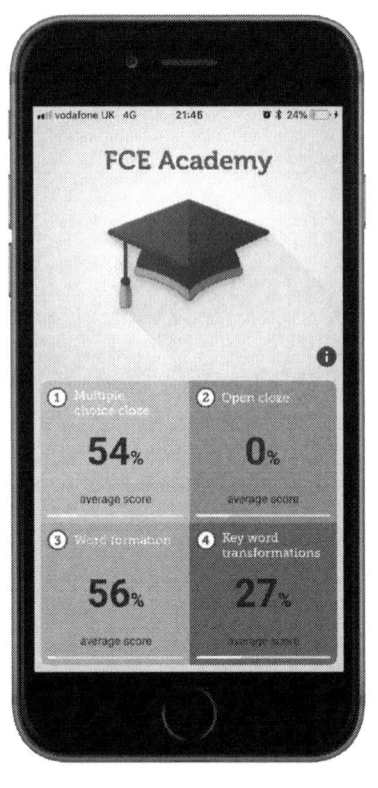

24	A	B	C
25	A	B	C
26	A	B	C
27	A	B	C
28	A	B	C
29	A	B	C
30	A	B	C

50% discount code: 050DAUQ0

Cambridge B2 First Listening

Answers — Test 1

Part 1							
1	A	2	A	3	B	4	B
5	C	6	C	7	B	8	A

Part 2	
9	football
10	travelling theatre group / theatre group / theatre company
11	musical performance / performance
12	TV commercial / commercial / ad / advert
13	networking
14	unemployment
15	too busy
16	social media
17	films / movies
18	strengths

Part 3					
19	C	20	B	21	A
22	H	23	E		

Part 4					
24	B	25	B	26	B
27	A	28	A	29	B
30	C				

Cambridge B2 First Listening

Answers — Test 2

Part 1							
1	A	2	B	3	A	4	B
5	C	6	C	7	A	8	B

Part 2	
9	cousin
10	Barcelona
11	lunch
12	flatmates / roommates
13	morning / mornings
14	grammar
15	lunch / long lunch / long lunches
16	the weekend / the weekends / weekends
17	write a letter / write
18	Economics

Part 3					
19	H	20	D	21	C
22	B	23	E		

Part 4					
24	B	25	C	26	A
27	C	28	A	29	A
30	B				

Cambridge B2 First Listening

Answers   Test 3

Part 1							
1	C	2	B	3	A	4	B
5	B	6	A	7	B	8	C

Part 2	
9	vet / zoo vet
10	glove / furry glove / big furry glove
11	Rwanda / Africa
12	hit / success
13	TV personality / personality
14	missing link
15	deer
16	dramatic
17	stop
18	humble / humbled / truly humble

Part 3					
19	F	20	B	21	G
22	E	23	D		

Part 4					
24	A	25	C	26	B
27	B	28	C	29	A
30	C				

Cambridge B2 First Listening

Answers

Test 4

Part 1

1	B	2	C	3	B	4	A
5	A	6	C	7	B	8	A

Part 2

9	Managing your time
10	pay
11	encourage / positively encourage
12	email
13	cry
14	attic
15	cat food
16	annoyed
17	angry
18	dog

Part 3

19	C	20	B	21	A
22	H	23	G		

Part 4

24	A	25	A	26	C
27	B	28	B	29	C
30	B				

Cambridge B2 First Listening

Answers Test 5

Part 1							
1	B	2	C	3	A	4	A
5	B	6	A	7	A	8	B

Part 2	
9	different
10	monitor / sports monitor / sport monitor
11	seven
12	Logistics / logistics
13	Health and Safety
14	military precision
15	printed list / list
16	reputation
17	paper animals
18	water fight

Part 3					
19	F	20	E	21	H
22	D	23	B		

Part 4					
24	C	25	B	26	B
27	A	28	A	29	C
30	B				

Cambridge B2 First Listening

Answers — Test 6

Part 1							
1	A	2	B	3	A	4	C
5	C	6	B	7	A	8	B

Part 2	
9	enthusiasm
10	daughter
11	remember
12	technique
13	London
14	two hours
15	10,000
16	forty-eight
17	fingering
18	listen to

Part 3					
19	A	20	E	21	H
22	D	23	B		

Part 4					
24	B	25	B	26	A
27	C	28	C	29	A
30	B				

Cambridge B2 First Listening

Answers Test 7

Part 1

1	C	2	B	3	A	4	A
5	C	6	C	7	B	8	C

Part 2

9	stereotype
10	crowded
11	ferry
12	inexperienced
13	priority
14	injure
15	strong current / current
16	physically fit
17	washing-up liquid / a special comb
18	different

Part 3

19	A	20	E	21	H
22	D	23	B		

Part 4

24	A	25	B	26	B
27	A	28	C	29	C
30	B				

Cambridge B2 First Listening

Answers — Test 8

Part 1

1	B	2	C	3	C	4	A
5	B	6	A	7	A	8	B

Part 2

9	full-time
10	an apprenticeship
11	university degree
12	1,500
13	10 / ten years
14	strange
15	lonely
16	different
17	travelling
18	understanding

Part 3

19	H	20	F	21	D
22	C	23	E		

Part 4

24	B	25	A	26	B
27	C	28	B	29	A
30	C				

Cambridge B2 First Listening

Answers — Test 9

Part 1

1	B	2	B	3	A	4	C
5	A	6	B	7	C	8	A

Part 2

9	natural
10	the countryside / countryside
11	ten minutes
12	into a lake
13	sunbathing
14	safety / his safety
15	very slowly / slowly
16	the cold / cold
17	parking
18	lunch / meal

Part 3

19	F	20	B	21	G
22	D	23	E		

Part 4

24	A	25	B	26	C
27	B	28	B	29	C
30	A				

Cambridge B2 First Listening

Answers — Test 10

Part 1

1	C	2	A	3	C	4	B
5	B	6	A	7	C	8	B

Part 2

9	the piano
10	teaching / teaching music
11	patience
12	musicianship
13	the keyboard / the piano
14	network
15	music fan / fan
16	fit / healthy / fit and healthy
17	Social Media
18	digital brand management

Part 3

19	H	20	G	21	E
22	F	23	C		

Part 4

24	B	25	C	26	A
27	C	28	A	29	B
30	A				

Transcripts   Test 1

Part 1

Audio track: FCE_Listening_1_1.mp3

FCE Academy, listening practice for the Cambridge English First FCE examination. As it is in the exam, each recording will be introduced and you will have time to read the questions before the recording is played. In the exam, you will hear each recording twice. At the beginning of each recording you will hear this sound: [tone]. It is good practice to write notes while you listen to each recording.

Part 1: You will hear people speaking in eight different situations. For questions 1–8, you must choose the best answer, A, B or C.

Question 1 You hear two people talking about the college canteen. How do they disagree?

[tone]

Girl: You know what? I think the canteen has really improved this term.

Boy: Well... the coffee is still great value for money, I'll say that for them.

Girl: And what about the staff? Nothing is too much trouble for them. You only have to ask.

Boy: Agreed. Mind you, the food still leaves a lot to be desired. The only thing I'd call edible are the sandwiches.

Girl: No way! You obviously haven't tried the lasagne. That new guy in the kitchen really knows his stuff. And those new pies are delicious.

[tone]

Question 2 You hear a woman talking about life skills. Where does she think the most valuable lessons are learned?

[tone]

One of the most valuable skills you'll learn in life is 'effective communication': how to explain your ideas to somebody to get what you want. Many people think that this skill is developed in adult life, for example, at university, or even through playing sports, but, actually, I think it is learned from an early age. The ability to get on with others is first learned in the relationship you have with your parents and brothers and sisters. This teaches children to be careful in what they say to others, learning the skills of persuasion as they go.

[tone]

Question 3 You hear an announcement at the airport. What problem is being explained?

[tone]

Passengers travelling on Scottish Airways flight number SA7921 to Portugal, please be advised that, due to adverse weather conditions, your departure is expected to be delayed. Passengers requiring further information should report to the Scottish Airways service desk. Though queues at security are expected to be no longer than usual, passengers are advised to check-in immediately and proceed to the departure lounge. Scottish Airways apologises for any inconvenience this delay may cause.

[tone]

Question 4   You hear a woman presenting on a TV show. What is she talking about?

[tone]

For birthdays and special occasions everyone loves one of these. The most important thing to remember when doing something like this is that you must always have everything you need *before* you start. First, get a good recipe. Read it well and find out what you'll need. Then, find a good shop that you know will have the necessary ingredients. After that you will need to get your utensils ready, such as: a baking tray, a mixing bowl and a wooden spoon. Before you mix the ingredients together, make sure that the oven is pre-heated so that you are not waiting around!

[tone]

Question 5   You hear two students talking about a teacher. How does the boy feel?

[tone]

Boy: Hi Grace.

Girl: Hi Ben, how are you doing?

Boy: Terrible. It's Mr Jack. I'm just not getting on with him.

Girl: What's the problem this time? Do you still think he doesn't like you?

Boy: It's not that. Not exactly. Anyway, I don't really care about that anymore.

Girl: But you were always so keen to impress your Maths teachers.

Boy: Not any more! I'm going right off it.

Girl: All because of Mr Jack? What has he done that's so bad that it has put you off your favourite subject?

Boy: He failed me on a quiz and I checked my answer later – it was definitely correct. I'm just not sure he knows what he's talking about, and therefore if he's doing a good job.

Girl: If I were you, I'd report that to the Principal. Get it sorted out as soon as you can.

[tone]

Question 6   You hear a football commentary on the radio. What is the reporter saying about the match?

[tone]

Who knows what the final score would have been? Both teams showed moments of great skill, and there was real excitement in the stadium throughout the first half, especially when the second goal was disallowed. The crowd was disappointed not to see the game continue after the break, especially as many had travelled a long way in the snow to be there. But the referee was right to call it off. The weather was just too bad to continue – it would have been dangerous for the players!

[tone]

Question 7   You overhear two friends who have just been to the cinema. What do they agree on?

[tone]

Woman: Well, I really enjoyed that despite all the bad reviews. It might have been a bit over-the-top, but what else do people expect from a big-budget action movie these days?

Man: I don't know. A plot that makes sense? Characterisation?

Woman: [laughs] So you didn't like it?

Man: No, I did not. I'm getting fed up of these Hollywood films anyway. I think games are the future of entertainment.

Woman: Not if you ask me. I love the cinema. The popcorn, the trailers, the whole thing. Mind you, it is rather an expensive evening.

Man: Too right. Cinema tickets are a complete rip-off!

[tone]

Question 8 You hear a man speaking on a telephone. What is he trying to do?

[tone]

Hello. I have been having trouble with your self-service ticket machine. I put in my dates of travel and ordered a single ticket to the city centre, but then the screen went blank. I tried again and the same thing happened. I need to get to my hotel where I'm meeting some friends. Is there anything you can do to help me? There is nobody here in the station to talk to and I have to get the next one or else I'll be late.

[tone]

Part 2

Audio track: FCE_Listening_1_2.mp3

Now turn to Part 2. You hear Dom Marcus, a professional actor, talking about his career. For questions 9–18, complete the sentences with a word or short phrase. You now have 45 seconds to look at Part 2.

[tone]

When I was in school I was interested in drama and loved all the school productions of famous plays and shows, but it wasn't taught as a subject until I was 13. By then I was really into sport, and football was definitely my favourite part of games. It wasn't until a travelling theatre group came to our school, when I was possibly 12 years old, that I really took notice and thought about being an actor.

By the time I was 18, I was studying English, Art and Drama and applied to Drama College in London and had to do an interview. I really loved it there, even though I found it hard at times, especially the musical performance part. Because I'm not a musician, I found that the most difficult aspect of the course: I just don't have natural rhythm! Thankfully, you can make it as an actor even if you're terrible at dancing and singing, like me, although that does limit your employment possibilities a bit.

My first actual job, once I'd finished my studies, was a TV commercial for dog food. I really love dogs, so this was a lot of fun to do. It was also a great learning experience as I got to understand more about the technical side of filming. A lot of people are involved in making a 60-second commercial – you'd be amazed!

After that first job, I was offered more work – it's true what they say: it's all about who you know. Networking is a very important part of an actor's lifestyle. From the outside, some people might think that actors are always partying, but, in fact, we are *networking*: making contacts and letting people know who you are is what it's all about.

Of course, there's a lot of disappointment, too, and long periods of time where you don't have any work. You need to be prepared for this as being rejected is a regular occurrence! Actors are also unemployed a lot of the time so they'll have other 'normal' jobs on the side, just to pay the rent. Thankfully, I'm now in a position where I have regular acting work. In fact, I have to turn down acting jobs because I'm so busy.

My daughter is 19 and is currently at university. I pay her to help with my social media – my Facebook and Twitter accounts and that sort of thing. It takes a lot of time just to keep on top of these, and it's extremely important that an actor has a social-media presence nowadays.

I definitely prefer doing TV work, like short drama series, as you film for just a couple of weeks and then you're finished. I've done a few feature-length movies. This is the type of work I like the least. They can be a little boring to work on, as much of your time is spent waiting around. A movie can be in filming for several months, and you need to be on set the whole time, even if your character only has a small part. But the pay is good for movies, so I probably shouldn't complain!

My advice for young actors looking to break into the industry? Well, I would say that you need to be prepared for failure and rejection, and being out of work, and that you must always keep positive: your break will come! It is important to know what your strengths are, and what you're *not* good at, and then to be working on these as much as you can. And it's always good to keep studying: there are loads of successful actors who offer master classes, and I have attended a few: you'll always learn something from experienced people.

[tone]

Part 3

Audio track: FCE_Listening_1_3.mp3

Now turn to Part 3. You hear five people talking about their student days. For questions 19–23, assign the correct speaker to the statement given. There are three extra options which you do not have to use. You now have 30 seconds to look at Part 3.

[tone]

Speaker 1 I was classified as a mature student when I started my course. I didn't feel it. I was only 25! Just having a few more years under my belt and, I suppose, that extra bit of life experience, made university a very different experience for me. Don't forget I'd held down a job for several years – even started building a career – and I had a long-term relationship and, by my third year, a baby to think about. Late nights but no parties. University felt more like a job that I had to do well. Not the three-year holiday it was for some of the other students.

Speaker 2 It took me some time to get into the swing of life at Uni. I grew up in a tiny town out in the middle of nowhere, so moving to a big city was a huge change for me. I eventually got down to studying, of course, but for those first few months I was in a complete whirlwind of parties, days on the beach, and the opposite sex. No wonder I couldn't concentrate on my work! A few bad marks brought me to my senses, though. I couldn't afford to waste the opportunity of Uni. And I knew I could relax once I'd got my degree.

Speaker 3 I lived in dorm my first year, and it was really difficult to work there. Most people find it difficult to focus when there's noise going on, and that dorm was completely chaotic. There was music morning, noon and night, and I'm not talking about soothing classical music you can tune out while you write your assignments. No, this was heavy rock, rap, R&B – and usually at least two stereos blasting out at one time. And just my luck – the life and soul of campus social life lived three doors down from me. Honestly, I was so relieved when it was time to find new accommodation.

Speaker 4 I didn't have a lot of money at university, and unfortunately that came to dominate the whole experience for me. It was really difficult to make ends meet from Day One: I had to work part-time just to get by. In my second year, I was working in a bar three nights a week and doing a couple of days as a bicycle courier. Juggling working and studying was incredibly difficult, and the worst of it is that I still have a massive student loan to pay off. It remains to be seen whether it's all been worth it.

Speaker 5 Many people think their life is like a straight road. They start at Point A and work through points B, C and D until they get to zee. My life hasn't been like that. When I was a kid I was very studious, always reading, and I figured I'd get good grades and go on to college to study. Problem is, once I got the grades and started, I realised I wasn't happy. I switched my major a couple of times before eventually dropping out. The only thing I really learned was what I *didn't* want to do. Still, you have to look on the bright side. I'm happy with my life now.

Part 4

Audio track: FCE_Listening_1_4.mp3

Now turn to Part 4. You hear an interview with a man called Raymond Osman, who works as a chiropractor in Madrid. For questions 24–30, choose the best answer, A, B or C. You will now have one minute to look at Part 4.

[tone]

My name's Raymond Osman, and I'm a chiropractor living in Madrid.

A chiropractor is someone who uses therapies such as massage to treat problems with joints and muscles. It's a complementary therapy, but it's well respected and requires several years of study before you can register as a practitioner. I have a masters degree which I earned in the UK before coming to Spain.

It could be seen as quite a strange career choice, especially speaking as someone from a family of academics, but I've always felt the urge to help people and I love the feeling of helping a patient to resolve an issue that they thought they'd never get rid of: chronic pain can seem like a prison sentence. My parents know I do valuable work and that I'm helping people, so they're proud of me.

What brought me to Spain? Well, my parents originally came from Barcelona, although they're very happy living in the UK, so I was always here in my school holidays and I spoke Spanish at home (although I'm told I have a very strange accent). And I love the place - and so does my wife, even though I think she misses her home in England more than I ever do. I'm incredibly lucky that there's such a demand for my services in Madrid. Plenty of work means I get to live in a place I love.

It's quite a varied job, especially as I've gradually built up a reputation for rehabilitating professional athletes. I work a lot with footballers, and I do some speaking at conferences. And I spend a lot of time learning and trying out new techniques, as well as treating a huge range of issues. It's the work with sports injuries I enjoy the most, and that's where I focus most of my efforts.

There are many reasons people come to see chiropractors. But when you get down to it, their problems have quite a limited range of causes. Bad diet is a big one – how can you feel well when you're filling your body with rubbish? And a lack of exercise leads to immobility, problems with joint pain and muscular issues. But a very common problem is people not getting around to addressing their symptoms early enough. If I could give one piece of advice it would be this: Don't ignore that niggling pain – the longer you leave it the more likely it is to become a chronic problem.

Mind you, if people caught their problems early, maybe I wouldn't be doing so well. Every cloud has a silver lining, as they say.

If I wanted to, I could work all day every day. But, actually, my practice with sportspeople means that I can choose my own hours to a certain extent. I have to work most mornings, but after that I tend to focus on other things in the afternoon before seeing a few more patients in the evening.

Now that I'm standing on my own two feet financially, and have paid off the loan I took out to start my own practice, of course I'm planning my next move. I'm never happy sitting on my laurels – I have to be looking forward to my next challenge. Right now I'm planning to set up my own chiropractic school here in Madrid. It's an expanding field, and more and more youngsters are considering it as a career. I can't wait to see my name over the door of a school!

[tone]

Transcripts

Test 2

Part 1

Audio track: FCE_Listening_2_1.mp3

FCE Academy, listening practice for the Cambridge English First FCE examination. As it is in the exam, each recording will be introduced and you will have time to read the questions before the recording is played. In the exam, you will hear each recording twice. At the beginning of each recording you will hear this sound: [tone]. It is good practice to write notes while you listen to each recording. You will hear people speaking in eight different situations.

Part 1: You will hear people speaking in eight different situations. For questions 1–8, you must choose the best answer, A, B or C.

Question 1 You hear an urban planning consultant talking about children's playgrounds in cities. What does she say about them?

[tone]

On average, the Department of Urban Planning receives one hundred planning applications every day, and they simply can't cope with the amount of work that's involved. Unfortunately, city councils need to prioritise their workload and kids' playgrounds often don't get the recognition they deserve. These areas are centres for the community, where mothers and fathers meet their neighbours and establish a community spirit, so they are important for adults as well as children. Safety standards are taken seriously and getting plans approved takes time. Gone are the days when one person could authorise a new plan, and getting a children's playground built involves a lengthy process.

[tone]

Question 2 You hear a man talking about being a teenager. What does he say about the experience?

[tone]

I was never a rebellious teenager, one of those kids who was always in trouble, but I wouldn't say I had a wonderful time of it. I didn't go through hell or anything - it was just that I was the quiet, shy type and it took me a while to find my feet. I guess, like most teens, I felt sorry for myself. Too many spots, not enough girlfriends, and of course my parents didn't understand me. I'm happy to say we never really fell out though. All the same – I wouldn't want to repeat those years. Being an adult is a much happier time.

[tone]

Question 3 You hear two people talking about the local bus service. What do they say about it?

[tone]

Man: Have you been waiting long?

Woman: Of course! This bus is always late. Better sit down – you'll be here for a while. My friend just texted me – they've only just got onto the main road.

Man: I knew I should have taken the train, but bus tickets are so much cheaper.

Woman: Well that's the one thing in its favour. But the bus always takes ages to arrive. And even when it comes, it still goes all around the houses before you get to town.

Man: Still, it probably means I'll save a bit of money over the course of the year.

Woman: You should get a season ticket. They're even better value.

Man: Look, here it comes!

[tone]

Question 4 You hear someone making an announcement about a TV schedule. What do they say?

[tone]

Due to the late start to the opening ceremony of the Olympic Games earlier today, which as you can see is still going on, we've had to rearrange tonight's schedule. If you've tuned in expecting to see this week's episode of 'Country Kitchen Time', I'm afraid you'll have to come back this time next week. Although if you really can't wait, this week's recipes are all on the web. Meanwhile, 'Five Guys in a Car' will be shown later than planned, at midnight. And if you want to catch that opening ceremony in full, the Olympics will be available on 'catch-up' all this week.

[tone]

Question 5 You hear two pupils discussing their recent exam results. What do they agree on?

[tone]

Girl: I'm glad that's over and done with. I never want to go through that again ... but I'm sure I'll have to resit the test.

Boy: Well, I probably got a pass. To be honest with you, I think I expected it to be a lot simpler so I didn't revise enough.

Girl: Well, from my point of view it was impossible. I'm sure we didn't cover all of those questions in class. We should complain about Mr Jill.

Boy: No, we can't complain – we'd definitely seen it all before. I'm sure if I'd done more revision I'd have remembered the topics better, that's all.

[tone]

Question 6 You hear a PE teacher speaking. What does he say about Sports?

[tone]

If I had it my way, Sports would be a higher priority subject in the school. I mean, who doesn't enjoy sport? Whether it's team games, like football or rugby, or individual sports, like tennis, there's something for everyone. It's just a shame the kids can't do more of it at school. Especially as a lot of them really need to keep fit. I can understand the constraints of the timetable but surely it's obvious that a healthy body makes a healthy mind. Kids who are physically active are better prepared for mental work. It's a fact.

[tone]

Question 7 You hear a painter talking about a photography course she went on. What does she say about it?

[tone]

I never saw it before, the relationship between painting and photography, but it's true. They say art imitates life, but I think that art *replicates* life. I always respected photographers in my circle of friends, and I always go to new photography exhibitions, but I never really understood that taking photos could be so much fun. I was really surprised by how much enjoyment I got from taking snaps of everything around me. Way more than what I get out of painting. I just wish I'd picked up a proper camera sooner: I'm now making up for lost time.

[tone]

Question 8   You hear a women talking about having just run a marathon. How does she say she feels?

[tone]

Am I disappointed not to have won? No, not at all! Just finishing is the reward. 12 months ago, I was what you'd call a 'casual runner'. I enjoyed it but enjoyed staying in watching TV more, especially in the winter months. But when I saw how much money could be raised through sponsorship, I became more and more focused. And the support I received from friends and colleagues was fantastic. Really amazing actually. I'm now a fitness fanatic. I run every day and it's exciting to think about what you can achieve if you put your mind to something. I know that's something people often say, but it's so true.

[tone]

Part 2

Audio track: FCE_Listening_2_2.mp3

Now turn to Part 2. You hear Mary Jones talking about a language course she went on. For questions 9–18, complete the sentences with a word or short phrase. You now have 45 seconds to look at Part 2.

[tone]

I had wanted to study Spanish for as long as I can remember. At school we did French and German, and I hated both. So when I was finally old enough and I had saved up enough money I decided to go to Spain and do an intensive Spanish course. I looked on the internet for details of courses, but as commonly happens it was someone in my circle of friends, my cousin in fact, who was actually able to give me the best information. She had previously done the same as I wanted to do, and she told me all about her wonderful experience. She had been to Madrid, the Spanish capital. She said it was wonderful, but a bit hot in the summer. I had visited Spain before but only the coast, which was much more touristy. I still wanted to have a beach, which Madrid doesn't, so finally I chose Barcelona – the capital of Catalonia in the northeast of Spain.

The language academy my cousin attended had a school in Barcelona. She said she'd had a great experience there so I called them up and booked on a three-month course. I arrived the day the course started – very early in the morning – and went straight to the academy. There was a welcome lunch and everyone on the course and all the teachers turned up. And there was a buffet and soft drinks. I suppose it was intended as a way to get to know people, and that is exactly what I did. There was one girl called Jill who I hit it off with straight away. Turns out she was looking for someone to share her newly rented flat with. After the lunch she invited me round to see the place and just like that we became flat mates! It was really fortunate for both of us actually. And the very next day we got down to studying. We opted for the early morning classes from 10–2, so as to have our afternoons free. The classes were great and we helped each other a lot. Jill could never remember the new vocabulary, but for me that was easy. It was grammar I really struggled with. We made a promise to only speak to each other in Spanish, despite the fact she is from the US and her first language is English, just like me.

What I loved more than anything, and it had never even crossed my mind before I came to Spain, was the wonderful long lunches, and I made sure I went for one every single day after studying. We really enjoyed the social life in Spain, too. We wanted to keep studying at the weekends also and so we went to 'intercambios' – culture and language exchanges. I was really surprised by the diversity of the people I met there. From all over the world. It was incredible. I had a wonderful time and the three months just flew by.

I'm back in the UK now. I did consider studying Spanish at university but since I didn't study it at school I didn't have the qualifications to get onto a uni course. So I'm doing Economics instead. I am, however, studying Spanish at night school, so who knows what will happen in the future. Jill and I made a promise to stay in contact. On Facebook as everyone does, but we also write a letter to each other once a month, in Spanish of course.

[tone]

Part 3

Audio track: FCE_Listening_2_3.mp3

Now turn to Part 3. You hear five people talking about their relationships with animals. For questions 19–23, assign the correct speaker to the statement given. There are three extra options which you do not have to use. You now have 30 seconds to look at Part 3.

[tone]

Speaker 1 I've always been crazy about teddy bears. Since I was a kid I have collected the stuffed creatures and I literally have about 200 hundred at home. I love any stories with them in it, and I sleep with one every night called Cuddles. I really am an animal lover. I am, believe it or not, actually studying Animal Behaviour at Uni, so I do know a lot about bears. I know in real life they are wild animals which could rip your arm off with one swipe, but I like my version more.

Speaker 2 It's irrational I know. There are no poisonous types in this country and there is absolutely no way they can harm me but I am really scared of them. I think it comes from my mother, in fact, who screams out whenever she sees one crawling up the wall or whenever finds a web somewhere. And my brother was always pulling our legs, putting fake spiders on our seats and things like that. He seems to find it entertaining to frighten us.

Speaker 3 People say never work with animals or children. For me, I leave the kids at home, but I choose to work – and really love working – with animals. I'm a puppy-raiser and trainer. For me, it's the best job in the world. It's dogs that I teach – dogs who will eventually work with the blind. They come to me when they are still puppies, but we don't start training them until they are over a year old. They stay with me throughout their training, but these animals are not pets. They are working dogs after all, and what they do for some people is just incredible.

Speaker 4 I do really like animals. Honestly I do, but I just can't be around them. I can't even go into a friend's house where there's a cat. I don't mind the smell or anything like that. I see people who have pets and I am really jealous. I'd love to learn to ride a horse but that is out of the question, too. My problem is that animals cause me to itch as soon as I am around them. My eyes get red and puffy and it's just so unpleasant I can't put up with it. The only thing to do is to keep away from them.

Speaker 5 I've been on the Force for about five years now. You need to do your first two years just like every other officer, but after that you can specialise. Some people go into the Traffic Police, others go in to Armed Response units. I actually grew up on a farm and riding horses was all part of my normal day. So it made sense to join the Mounted Police. You see us in crowds, such as outside football matches, town centres and parks. Horses gives us a vantage point and also add a visibility that we just wouldn't have without them.

Part 4

Audio track: FCE_Listening_2_4.mp3

Now turn to Part 4. You hear Colin Tracton, a sports scientist from Upton University. For questions 24–30, choose the best answer, A, B or C. You will now have one minute to look at Part 4.

[tone]

Interviewer: I am joined this evening by Colin Tracton, a sports scientist from Upton University. Welcome Colin.

Colin: Thanks for having me Jim.

Interviewer: Tell us about what attracted you to Upton University in the first place?

Colin: Well, actually it was a bit of a trek from home. I'm from up north so it meant I had to move here instead of staying with my parents. This university has the best Track and Field team in the country and that is why, basically, I decided I wanted to come here. I had been offered a scholarship at another uni and turned it down, which some people would think was crazy, but my father was very supportive and wanted the best for me and my then-promising sports career. I really wanted to be part of the Upton team.

Interviewer: You mention your sports career – you're a renowned academic now, but I understand you had a tough break as far as your own sports career was involved.

Colin: Unfortunately I did. I was a middle-distance runner. I was doing really well. I had won a medal in the national junior championships and hoped to compete internationally as a professional athlete. Then one day I was involved in a terrible crash while travelling as a passenger in a car. I spent two months in hospital and the surgeon told me I was lucky to be able to walk again. I'm OK now, but I never fully recovered to the level I was at before.

Interviewer: That's terrible Colin. You got back to uni though, didn't you, and completed your course successfully. What did you do as the theme for your final project?

Colin: Well, lots of people were doing things about nutrition and about how certain foods might react with your body and all that. I am interested in that, too, but I chose to investigate a new type of exercise called High Intensity Interval Training which was just becoming popular at the time. I was doing the work just as it was coming into the public eye and it was getting a bit of interest.

Interviewer: So much interest in fact that you decided to continue studying – going on to get your masters and eventually your doctorate. How did that come about?

Colin: Well, as part of a project set up by the uni we wanted to go out and interact with the public, so we ended up in a shopping centre getting members of the public to try this type of exercise out. A national TV channel heard about it and came to do an article on us for the Good Morning UK show. I got the opportunity to speak on camera and became a bit of a celebrity on the show. It was really weird. They started paying me in fact, and people would call in to ask me questions. I felt terribly lacking in knowledge and thought it would be a great idea to keep studying. The uni was really pleased by the exposure it was getting on the show and welcomed me with open arms!

Interviewer: So tell us about this remarkable new fitness method. It says here you can do it in just five minutes, three times a week. Is that correct? Is this some type of cheat to getting fit for lazy people?

Colin: Certainly not, Jim. You need to make the effort, just as with any exercise, but it's true that it requires less time than most methods.

Interviewer: So how does it work then? What's the trick?

Colin: There is no trick – it's all about stimulating the areas of the body related to breathing and getting your muscles working. It works quickly and effectively. You can achieve what you would by sweating in the gym for an hour in just a few minutes every day.

Interviewer: That's seems too good to be true, Colin. But you do go into the science behind it in your new book....... (fade)

[tone]

Transcripts   Test 3

Part 1

Audio track: FCE_Listening_3_1.mp3

FCE Academy, listening practice for the Cambridge English First FCE examination. As it is in the exam, each recording will be introduced and you will have time to read the questions before the recording is played. In the exam, you will hear each recording twice. At the beginning of each recording you will hear this sound: [tone]. It is good practice to write notes while you listen to each recording.

Part 1: You will hear people speaking in eight different situations. For questions 1–8, you must choose the best answer, A, B or C.

Question 1 You hear someone speaking on the phone to a friend who has just failed her driving test. What is she doing?

[tone]

Well – I'm one to talk! You know I can't drive either. If you want to quit then I can't stop you, but you told me you need the car to take the kids to school. You'd be letting yourself down, and the kids. It's going to be a real inconvenience if you can't have the car by the start of the school year. Think about it. Two hours on the bus every day will be really tiring for the kids, too.

[tone]

Question 2 You hear a mother speaking with her daughter who is unable to come home for the weekend. How is the mother feeling?

[tone]

Don't worry about it, darling. It's not like you to call something off like this and I know you're not making up excuses. It's not a disappointment. Not at all. I can remember when I had exams you know! Look, I'll just pack up the car and come down to *you* instead. How about that? Some of my cooking will help you concentrate on your exams next week. I'll do my special pasta bake – we can eat it with your roommate, Stella. I really don't mind, my love. I'm your mother, after all.

[tone]

Question 3 You overhear two friends who have just watched a movie in the cinema. What do they agree was good about it?

[tone]

Man: Well, Tim Cream won't be winning any awards for *that* performance.

Woman: Don't you think so? I thought he was great.

Man: You think he is great in anything.

Woman: [laughs] Get off, you! But the special effects were really impressive, weren't they?

Man: Definitely. They were absolutely brilliant. But what about that script? It was terrible.

Woman: Yeah. Maybe not one of Tom's best moments.

[tone]

Question 4 You hear two people speaking about smartphones. What point does the woman make?

[tone]

Man: I think action needs to be taken. Children should absolutely not be allowed phones in school.

Woman: But what can you do about it? Parents want children to have them. They're just so useful.

Man: I don't think it matters. Teachers need to object. They didn't have them in my day.

Woman: I know. But they didn't have computers or cell phones either. These devices can be a calculator, a watch, allow instant internet access, and there are so many apps now. They're absolutely essential, I'd say.

Man: Well, I think too much time on those screens is bad for your health. and we just become over-reliant on them.

Woman: I see what you mean, but it's all about moderation...

[tone]

Question 5 You hear a teacher speaking to a student about their request to wear shorts in school. What is he saying?

[tone]

Teacher: You asked me yesterday and I told you 'no', and I have no reason to change my mind.

Student: But sir, it's even hotter than yesterday – it's boiling!

Teacher: I'm hot, you're hot, we're all hot – but that doesn't change the rules, now – does it, Steven?

Student: Please sir! My friend goes to Long Road School, and they are allowed to wear shorts in summer. It's not like you learn better just because you are in trousers.

Teacher: Well, maybe next year you can go to Long Road, too, and give me some peace and quiet. Now get on with your work, Steven.

[tone]

Question 6 You hear two students talking about preparing an essay. What are they both unsure about?

[tone]

Student A: So, how is that essay we have to hand in by Monday going? Do you think you'll get it finished?

Student B: Yeah – no problem. You?

Student A: Almost done. But do we have to include *all* the references?

Student B: Well I'm not sure. Can't we look it up somewhere?

Student A: Actually, it's all here on the website. It says 'reference everything you quote from a primary or secondary source. You should credit photos, too.'

Student B: But what about the internet? Do we have to credit website addresses, or the writers or what?

Student A: I have no idea. I'll ask Mr Harvey tomorrow.

[tone]

Question 7 You hear a tannoy announcement at a sports day. What is the speaker saying?

[tone]

Attention all race day spectators. Due to the terrible weather this morning, the Fun Run will now take place at the later time of 2pm, weather-permitting. Fun-runners can still join in by adding their names to the list in the Welcome Tent. The food area will open at lunchtime, but because of the weather all food trucks will now be situated inside the main tent instead of outside, as previously planned.

[tone]

Question 8   You hear a waiter speaking about his customers from the previous night. What does he say about them?

[tone]

Honestly, I thought I'd seen it all. But last night was definitely the worst. I've never been treated so badly by one table. It was as if they thought I wasn't a human being, the way they behaved. And I don't care who you are: manners don't cost anything. No matter what the situation, it's just not acceptable in my book. Showing a little respect is the least you can do, whoever you are. And as for their tip – they can keep it!

[tone]

Part 2

Audio track: FCE_Listening_3_2.mp3

Now turn to Part 2. You hear Karen Smart talking about her job as a wildlife TV presenter. For questions 9–18, complete the sentences with a word or short phrase. You now have 45 seconds to look at Part 2.

[tone]

How did I get started? Well, that's a long story. There was a long-running show in the 80s which profiled different jobs – one job a week. So, you'd get musicians, engineers, writers – all walks of life. I was working as a zoo vet in London at the time and they came to the zoo and followed me around with a camera as I looked after the animals. I was lucky – one of the sick animals was a baby gorilla and the public just latched on to the story. She was pretty sick, poor little mite, but I managed to save her by persuading her to take medicine from a bottle. I actually put on a big furry glove so she'd trust me more, which looked pretty funny. When the programme aired it attracted a lot of attention. I did a couple of radio and TV interviews off the back of that, and then I got offered a show by a little independent company in which I went to Rwanda to help care for the mountain gorillas there. I had a great time doing that, but I never thought that I was starting a new career. I thought I'd just go back to doing my thing after the show was over, but little did I know – it was a hit! We topped the ratings week after week, but because I was in the middle of Africa at the time I didn't really understand the impact it was making back home. I left England a zoo vet and came back a TV personality. Anyway, one thing led to another and pretty soon I was in high demand for presenting wildlife documentaries. Penguins, meerkats, dolphins – I've done the lot! My absolute favourite was the show where I went to Sumatra looking for the 'orang pendek'. It's a legendary creature there – kind of like their version of the abominable snowman or Bigfoot, a missing link between humans and apes. Of course, we never found one, although there was some tantalising evidence and I spoke to several locals who claimed to have seen one. One guy even showed me a photo on his mobile phone, but it could have been anything! Anyway, what we did find was a completely new kind of deer! Sumatra is still wild enough to hide unknown animals. So that was a bit of a bonus. Right now I'm just recording the voiceover for a programme on British wildlife. It's kind of a safari around an English woodland in the winter months. Our local animals may not be as picturesque as their African equivalents, but their lives are just as dramatic. Believe me, there's nothing more emotional than seeing a squirrel trying to survive a harsh winter, or a fox look after her cubs in a deep snow, or even the simple hedgehog hunting for worms in the undergrowth after a hard frost. It's incredible what these ordinary creatures do to get by. I think human life would just stop in such difficult conditions, but these little animals just keep on going. Incredible. And I think it's the animals that keep you grounded. I feel truly humble before them. However famous I get, it's the animals that are the real stars.

[tone]

Part 3

Audio track: FCE_Listening_3_3.mp3

Now turn to Part 3. You hear five people talking about their summer holidays. For questions 19–23, assign the correct speaker to the statement given. There are three extra options which you do not have to use. You now have 30 seconds to look at Part 3.

[tone]

Speaker 1 We work hard all year round and when it comes to vacations I really just want to be taken care of and relax. It's not really intentional, but when it comes time to book up for our break it's the same place we always want to go. So we do – year after year. We know everyone there and they know us. We know how much we will spend and know that it will always be just what we are looking for. If something isn't broke, why fix it?!

Speaker 2 I like all sorts of holidays. This year I went on a beach holiday. Last year, though, we went to Milan and Rome – big cities. I've gone backpacking and I've travelled all over the world. I must admit I really don't like holidays with loads of kids around. That's for two reasons. The first is they are really noisy – annoying if we are trying to relax on a beach or by a pool. And the second reason is really just because I like doing things like going to museums if I'm in the city, or restaurants and clubs. Kids don't really find all that very interesting and often misbehave.

Speaker 3 It's my idea of heaven: relaxing, switching off and being transported to exotic locations. And everything is done for you. You have a wide choice of restaurants so you never have to eat the same thing twice. And there is a formal dining room, and people tend to get dressed up in their fancy clothes to eat there. And of course the captain and all the officers are there in their uniforms. There is an amazing range of entertainment, too. Cinemas, bands, dance classes, and really good clubs for kids. All on board this kind of self-contained city.

Speaker 4 We have a big family and although my husband does help I don't think he realises how much work I put in all year round at home. So, what I like to do, and thankfully the kids do too, is go on a holiday where we only need the clothes we take in our suitcases, nobody needs to do any housework, and no-one has to cook. One of those holidays with everything thrown in is just what I need. We have been on several different ones – resorts that have pools, games, entertainment, bars and restaurants, and you can use the facilities just as much as you like. They give you a plastic card and they just scan it when you want something. For us, it really is the best holiday option.

Speaker 5 My idea of hell is spending a whole year working to then go and vegetate by a pool for two weeks. I know package holidays are great for some people, but not for me. I need stimulation and excitement and trying new things. I start off with a plan of what I want to see and do, but I never make plans for how I'm going to travel or where I am going to stay. Last year I arrived in Thailand with just my backpack. I knew where I wanted to end up and the date I needed to get back to the airport, but everything in between was to be an adventure. The more people I could meet and the more surprises I could find, the better.

Part 4

Audio track: FCE_Listening_3_4.mp3

Now turn to Part 4. You hear an interview with a woman called Sally Jones, a traveller who has recently returned from Ethiopia. For questions 24–30, choose the best answer, A, B or C. You will now have one minute to look at Part 4.

[tone]

Interviewer: Welcome to another episode of 'Suitcase Stories', which this time meets a traveller who has been to a most unusual holiday destination: Ethiopia. Welcome Sally Jones. How did you end up in Ethiopia?

Sally: I guess it is a bit strange, but I love going to relatively unknown places. I can't stand getting somewhere and realising every other person is a tourist. I went to Vietnam and the cities were full of holidaymakers. It was so depressing. But I honestly haven't met another traveller who has been to Ethiopia – so I thought, why not? I went during September, when the countryside is in full bloom after the hot summer and rainy season.

Interviewer: Is it difficult getting there?

Sally: Not especially, but getting around the country is difficult. As you'd expect, a lot of the roads are in a terrible condition. Bumps, ruts, abandoned roadworks, mud, floods – I saw the lot! They recommend only travelling during daylight because there are no lights on the road and a lot of livestock wander around at night. It's an accident waiting to happen. Even in daylight, travelling a short distance takes hours. And, I've just got to be honest, the buses are a nightmare.

Interviewer: And what makes the travel worthwhile?

Sally: The scenery is fantastic. People think it's a big dry country but actually there are beautiful forests, huge mountains with snow on the peaks, and enormous rivers. It's a very high country, too, so you get this wonderful quality of light during the day. And there's something new around every corner. But one of the best things is the coffee – it's absolutely delicious. Ethiopia is actually where people began drinking coffee and it somehow tastes different there – almost fruity.

Interviewer: What are the towns like? I've heard about the rock churches...

Sally: There are lots of those in the city of Lalibela – literally carved out of stone. Incredible. There's another city called Aksum which has these enormous stone pillars. And another called Gondar with beautiful castles and churches. They're more recent though – from the 17th century. I guess I didn't associate Ethiopia with beautiful architecture, but it's all there! You can take a tour of the northern cities – it's something they recommend in all the travel guidance.

Interviewer: Did anything else surprise you?

Sally: Yes! I've become quite an expert on surprising things about Ethiopia. Here's one: Did you know Ethiopia is the second oldest Christian country in the world? There have been Christians there since the fourth century. That's where all the churches come from. What else? Oh yes! They have their own time. Literally. The day starts at 6AM. That has to be the strangest thing you've heard, right? Oh, and they have their own alphabet that nobody else in the world uses.

Interviewer: Fascinating! And are the people welcoming?

Sally: Absolutely, yes. The country has a real image problem, but they're trying to build a tourist industry. Okay, maybe the accommodation isn't 100% up to scratch, but that will come. And, like most developing countries, you have to be a little bit careful about the food and drink. Some of the dishes are a bit, um, surprising! And there is still a lot of poverty, sadly, and you see this wherever you go. But the important thing is how friendly the people are. I'm definitely going back one day.

[tone]

Transcripts

Test 4

Part 1

Audio track: FCE_Listening_4_1.mp3

FCE Academy, listening practice for the Cambridge English First FCE examination. As it is in the exam, each recording will be introduced and you will have time to read the questions before the recording is played. In the exam, you will hear each recording twice. At the beginning of each recording you will hear this sound: [tone]. It is good practice to write notes while you listen to each recording.

Part 1: You will hear people speaking in eight different situations. For questions 1–8, you must choose the best answer, A, B or C.

Question 1 You hear two friends talking about a new computer. What does the man say about it?

[tone]

Woman: That's a nice laptop, Brian. When did you get that?

Man: I just picked it up yesterday. My old one broke and I had to get another one the next day. I need it for everything: college, my music – I can't live without it.

Woman: It looks fancy.

Man: It's a good one, but not the newest model.

Woman: Was it expensive?

Man: Actually, I was really lucky. There was a great sale on. It was a bargain.

[tone]

Question 2 You hear two friends discussing a play. What do they agree on?

[tone]

Woman A: You could have forgotten you were in a theatre sometimes, the backgrounds were so realistic.

Woman B: Maybe they should have spent less on the scenery and more on rehearsals. The actors kept forgetting their lines.

Woman A: Well I can sympathise with that. The acting wasn't bad. It was just so long. I don't think anyone can concentrate for such a long time.

Woman B: Definitely. I almost fell asleep.

Woman A: Almost? (laughs) I heard you snoring!

[tone]

Question 3 You hear a man talking about his new job. What does he say?

[tone]

So, the pay isn't too bad I suppose. It's better than what I was getting before. It's just such a different job. I'm going to have to get used to it, and that will take time. But I'm happier now. And my work/life balance is much better, too: I left my last job because of how it interfered with my family life. And I need to remember this as it's way more important not to be bringing your work home with you. I definitely won't do that again, no matter how much pressure I am under.

[tone]

Question 4 You hear a woman comparing train travel and air travel. What does she say?

[tone]

It depends how far you have to travel, of course. But, yes, definitely when it comes to reducing the stress of travelling, they are better. I know people say air travel is the better option, but I think it's often the least convenient. I think they have this glamourous idea that really isn't true anymore – especially with all those budget airlines. With security you need to arrive two hours before you fly. At the station it's 30 minutes before. Much better. And I need to be able to relax and stretch my legs, and use my laptop with an internet connection. You can do all that travelling by rail. Basically, I need to be able to do the things I would be doing if I wasn't travelling, like making phone calls and writing emails. In a plane, you're really limited all the while you're in the air.

[tone]

Question 5 You hear a woman talking about the new restaurant on the high street. What did she enjoy?

[tone]

It's fancy, and a bit too pricey for me, but it *was* my birthday. The decor is not my cup of tea, mind you, but I can see why people will like it there. Lots of natural light and cream colours – it's a very relaxing atmosphere. And the food? Well, not to everyone's taste, but I finished my plate. I think it's a mix of different styles of cooking – 'fusion' I think they call it. If it hadn't been a bit spicy I wouldn't have liked it at all.

[tone]

Question 6 You a hear a man talk about buying a new suit. What does he usually wear?

[tone]

I've got to get a new suit for my little brother's wedding and he's been clear that I've got to look smart but not 'smart/casual'. Whatever that means. The thing is, me and suits just don't get on! I hate feeling so rigid and formal – it makes me think of my dad. He has lots of suits, they're nearly all identical. Me? I'd rather be in my tracksuit. The closest thing to wearing a suit for me is when I put on my swimsuit! But I'll do the right thing for my brother's big day. I don't have much choice!

[tone]

Question 7 You hear a woman asking for directions. What advice is she given?

[tone]

Woman: Excuse me. I seem to be a bit lost. Could you help me?
Man: Eh, sure. Where are you going?

Woman: I'm looking for Telford Road. My sister lives there.

Man: OK, Just give me a minute. I have an app on my phone ... Here it is, but I'm afraid it's miles away!

Woman: Oh dear.

Man: Well, you can't walk it, that's for sure. Not in this weather.

Woman: I just want to get there as quickly as I can.

Man: If I were you I'd just jump in a cab. It'll only be about 5 pounds. There's a rank just here.

[tone]

Question 8 You hear a doctor giving advice over the phone to a patient. What instructions does he give?

[tone]

At your appointment yesterday I made it clear there wasn't a lot I could do, and Accident and Emergency is not for this sort of thing. They'd probably just send you home. You know how busy it is there. I think you are over-reacting. It's just a cold. We can't prescribe antibiotics for such complaints, I'm afraid. What you need is a good rest. A decent night's sleep will do wonders for you, I promise. You definitely can't just rush off to hospital, okay?

[tone]

Part 2

Audio track: FCE_Listening_4_2.mp3

Now turn to Part 2. You hear Caspian Ventura talk about his career as a freelance editor. For questions 9–18, complete the sentences with a word or short phrase. You now have 45 seconds to look at Part 2.

[tone]

The hardest thing about working as a freelance editor is getting used to not knowing what you'll be working on next. You go from job to job, most of the time, but sometimes you'll work on several different jobs at once. Managing your time, therefore, is really important. Managing your accounts is also crucial as clients can often take ages to pay you your hard earned money! You need to submit your invoice as soon as you've finished a piece of work because it will usually be 30 days before you get paid. So, it takes a while to get used to this way of working, and it helps if you have some savings set aside. But there are many benefits of being a freelance editor, and I would positively encourage anyone considering it as a career to go for it.

Firstly, you get to work on a wide range of materials. For example, one day you could be writing a newspaper article about elephants and the next day you'd be editing a fictional story about aliens invading Earth! You also get to work with interesting people, from the people who work for publishers to authors from all over the world. You'll have to attend meetings, and, occasionally, you'll be invited to special events, like book launches, but mostly, you'll communicate by email.

My favourite aspect of the job is getting to see the look on an author's face when they see their finished book for the first time. It can take them years to get to that point, and they'll be very grateful to you for the help you provide. More than once I've seen an author cry when they were handed a copy of their book. It's an emotional experience!

I've been working as a freelance editor for ten years and I'm always learning new things. My library is now huge and contains a very bizarre mix of books I have had to read. I have books on diverse subjects, from philosophy to applied mathematics, from religion to astrophysics, and lots of magazines and scraps of materials I've collected over the years. In fact, I have to keep them all upstairs in the attic, as there is just no room in my study any more. When I start a new project, I spend a great deal of time familiarising myself with the subject matter. Sometimes this means I have to learn about something completely new to me, like when I edited an entire book on cat food. That was actually the weirdest book I've ever done! I didn't know much about the subject but now I'm quite the expert! Sometimes, I annoy my friends by having something to say about most things – I can't help myself if I happen to know, for example, who the president of Djibouti is!

As a result of my work I can't read anything without spotting spelling mistakes or grammatical errors. It's amazing just how many mistakes end up being published – especially in newspapers where the production process is so fast. Sometimes I'll have to stop reading something if there are more than a handful of errors. It just gets me angry!

But let me finish on a positive note. Another benefit to working freelance, for me, has been that I've been able to get a dog, something I just couldn't do when I worked in an office. Because I am at home during the day, I can go for long dog walks whenever I want to and my dog can sit with me while I work. We enjoy each other's company and our shared lifestyle: I wouldn't change it for the world.

[tone]

Part 3

Audio track: FCE_Listening_4_3.mp3

Now turn to Part 3. You hear five people talking about their boss. For questions 19–23, assign the correct speaker to the statement given. There are three extra options which you do not have to use. You now have 30 seconds to look at Part 3.

[tone]

Speaker 1 Working with Bob is so familiar to me I think it would really be difficult to ever change. He has known me since I was at school. I was in his son's class and when I left school and I wanted to get on an apprenticeship to become an electrician Bob said he would take me on. After getting my qualifications I felt I owed it to him to continue working for him, at least for a while. That was twelve years ago and I'm still here. Spending so much time with Bob is great, but I do enjoy getting away from him on holiday when the time comes.

Speaker 2 Knowing the hard skills is essential, but nowadays you need to know something about what they call the soft skills, too. Getting the best out of your staff is about good people skills and Mr Jackson is lacking in those. I'm not saying he does it intentionally, but he does change what he says from day to day. I think he just forgets actually. There is no doubt he works really hard, but he doesn't really know how to delegate responsibility. That's the bigger problem: he can't allow anyone else to do the really important things. And that's just not good for the team.

Speaker 3 Jane is one of the hardest working people I know. She lives the job and has the most positive outlook I have seen. She never lets things get on top of her: she is extremely well organised and makes the sacrifices necessary to be a top manager. I just couldn't do it. And I wouldn't want to either. Ten years of 16-hour working days and a divorce to show for it. I know she is successful, and has the nice car and house, but it's just not worth it.

Speaker 4 It's not just the day-to-day work my boss does. It's also the extra things she does that make me look up to her, like remembering people's birthdays, or their children's names. Feeling that your boss genuinely cares makes you care about them, and, in turn, about your work. And I don't think those are skills you can learn. You either have it or you don't. Basically, she's a born leader and an inspiration in the workplace.

Speaker 5 A famous business leader once said 'always be nice to the nerds in your class because you will probably end up working for them'. A funny quote, but it wasn't so funny when I went for an interview and Paul greeted me as I arrived. I thought I may as well just go home then and there. Thankfully I didn't, and Paul was actually really nice to me, and he gave me the job. He did bring up that we used to joke about his height in school, but he didn't seem to remember the time someone locked him in a cupboard. Maybe he never knew it was me!

Part 4

Audio track: FCE_Listening_4_4.mp3

Now turn to Part 4. You hear a radio interview with a street musician called Mike McShane. For questions 24–30, choose the best answer, A, B or C. You will now have one minute to look at Part 4.

[tone]

Interviewer: Hi folks. Colin Fish here. I'm joined today by Mike McShane and he's here to talk to us about busking. He earns a living from playing live music, but not your usual concert halls or music venues! What makes busking different from other types of musical performance, Mike?

Mike: Busking is the name we give to playing music in the street. Well, actually it could be on the underground, in a park, or any public place where you just turn up and play, and the hope is that members of the public will give you money to show their appreciation.

Interviewer: So, how did you get started on a career as a busker?

Mike: I've been a busker for twelve years now. Anyone can busk, I suppose, but you are supposed to get permission. I have a performer's licence which I got by auditioning for a panel of judges when I started. That gives you the right to play in certain places at certain times. If you don't have this licence the police could fine or even arrest you.

Interviewer: And so do you need any special skills to get that licence?

Mike: It's all down to the audition. And anyone can have a go. If the panel likes you – you are granted a licence.

Interviewer: And so they obviously liked you. What preparation did you do for your audition?

Mike: Well, years of study in fact. Some people are surprised by the fact I attended music college. I actually studied piano there, though I play the guitar and sing when I'm performing nowadays.

Interviewer: Wow! So why did you decide to become a busker?

Mike: Busking can be a pretty irregular income. But if you put in the hours you can get by. I hated the thought of becoming a music teacher in a school. I always thought teaching would be boring. So this way I get to perform all day long. I love it!

Interviewer: Can you describe a normal day for you?

Mike: I play for eight hours, five days a week – just like a normal job. And just like a normal job, you have good days and bad days of course. Friday to Sunday are my busiest days. On Mondays everyone has the blues and never gives you any money, and Tuesdays are almost as bad – so I stay at home on those days. I have several places where I play. By far my favourite is in the underground system. It's warm and safe - mostly. They have allocated places to play and you need to use a booking system online to reserve your time.

Interviewer: And is it seasonal work?

Mike: Without a doubt Christmas is the best time of the year for busking. But you really need to be inside due to the weather. I sometimes play with other buskers, which I really enjoy, but then you have to share the money you earn. I do the odd concert with bands, but there is no serious money to be made there. I just do it for fun.

[tone]

Transcripts   Test 5

Part 1

Audio track: FCE_Listening_5_1.mp3

FCE Academy, listening practice for the Cambridge English First FCE examination. As it is in the exam, each recording will be introduced and you will have time to read the questions before the recording is played. In the exam, you will hear each recording twice. At the beginning of each recording you will hear this sound: [tone]. It is good practice to write notes while you listen to each recording.

Part 1: You will hear people speaking in eight different situations. For questions 1–8, you must choose the best answer, A, B or C.

Question 1 You hear two locals speak about tourists in their town. What do they agree on?

[tone]

Man A: I know it's easy to get fed up with so many tourists, but you have to look for the positive.

Man B: What's that? The rubbish they leave? The noise they make? I don't dislike the people, just the disruption they cause.

Man A: This town was so run down before the tourists started coming. Now there are jobs for everyone.

Man B: I can't argue with that. My shop *is* doing rather well, isn't it.

Man A: We should show some respect for these people.

[tone]

Question 2 You hear a professional soccer player talking about her last match. How does she feel?

[tone]

It was probably the worst match of my career. Yeah, and that would go for everyone else on the team, too! What a disaster, from start to finish. I'm just glad we were so fortunate in the end with that late penalty, which put us in the lead. 90th minute – no pressure at all! I can see why the referee isn't very popular, though. He didn't make any friends today. But that's soccer. You can't be everywhere at the same time and some things you'll miss.

[tone]

Question 3 You hear an announcement about public transport. What does it say?

[tone]

This is a service announcement. Passengers should be aware that from the 11th of June there will be a temporary change to allow for works on the northbound line. The last train will leave Queen's Street Station at 22:00 each evening and not resume until 6am the following morning. Replacement bus services will be in place for the next two months and will leave from outside the station. Please consult timetables in the station or online.

[tone]

Question 4 You hear a travel agent receiving a complaint from a customer over the phone. What is the problem?

[tone]

Woman: I'm just back from one of your package tours. In Alicante.
Man: Ah, yes! How was it?
Woman: Well, The weather was terrible.
Man: Oh, what a pity. It's usually better at this time of year.
Woman: I can cope with a bit of rain. Although it did mean we couldn't use the pool.
Man: Well, I'm sorry to hear that.
Woman: Not to worry. But I'm afraid I have to make a complaint. The problem is that when we booked the holiday with you we requested somewhere with child-friendly entertainment. There was hardly any entertainment at all, never mind it being child-friendly. They were bored to death.
Man: Okay. Let me take your details. What was your name again, madam?

[tone]

Question 5 You hear an answering machine message. What is the women saying about the school pick-up today?

[tone]

Hello. This is Elaine Thomas, Eliza and Pablo's mother. I'm calling to let you know I'm not going to be able to make the after-school pick-up today. I usually collect both kids but their grandmother will be coming today as I've had to go in to work unexpectedly and won't be home until later. You can reach her on her mobile, if there's any problem. You should have the number in your records. And you have my details, of course, just in case. If I don't answer it's because I'm in a meeting, and I'll call you straight back. Thanks so much.

[tone]

Question 6 You hear a street musician. Which music does he enjoy playing most?

[tone]

If it were up to me I'd be playing the music I'm best at. After all, I'm a classically trained guitarist. But that's not what the people want to hear. You've got to play the old favourites: the catchy songs that everyone knows. Pop music, basically. If you want to earn the big bucks, it's got to be what's popular, even if that's not what you're into. I also have to be careful not to get too rocky either as some people don't react well to that. It's all about playing things that are familiar to the public.

[tone]

Question 7 You hear someone speaking on the phone. What is wrong with the trousers?

[tone]

I know what he says, but that's ridiculous: they couldn't have shrunk. And of course I haven't washed them. They still have the ticket on. They're just too tight. I can't do them up. Yes – they do say large, and that is what I ordered, but they just don't fit. Yes that's right – exchange them – that's right. I've been saying this for the last 5 minutes!

[tone]

Question 8 You hear a weather forecast. What will the weather be like tomorrow?

[tone]

Tomorrow's weather will be largely overcast with some scattered showers across the region. It's not going to be a day for the beach, that's for sure. At least it won't be as bad as it's going to be at the start of next week, when it looks like it will be turning very wintry with temperatures falling to –2 or even –3 degrees in some areas. These conditions are unusual for this time of year, and we are in for one of the coldest Aprils in recent memory.

[tone]

Part 2

Audio track: FCE_Listening_5_2.mp3

Now turn to Part 2. You hear Sebastian, a children's summer camp director, talking about his job. For questions 9–18, complete the sentences with a word or short phrase. You now have 45 seconds to look at Part 2.

[tone]

Hi. I'm Sebastian and I am the director of a summer camp for children. I've actually worked for the same school for my entire career as a teacher. It's called Queen's College. During the year I work at the normal school. Then, in July we run the summer camp. The children who come in July are not the same pupils who come all year round. They just sign up for the month.

I have worked as a teacher, camp coordinator and sub-director before finally getting my current job. I actually started off as a sports monitor during my first summer here, while I was studying at university. When I graduated it didn't cross my mind to work anywhere else, and as a member of staff was retiring that year I applied for her job. Thankfully I always got on well with the team and they knew me, so I got my first full-time job as a teacher. I progressed through the school and now I have a camp of my own. It only took five years from that first part-time appointment as a monitor. And I've been here for a further two now.

The most challenging aspect of the course isn't the children, or the parents – although they are difficult to deal with, too. In fact, it's the logistics: moving people and things from A to B. On the first day of camp around 160 children arrive. The only ones we know are children from previous years' camps. We need to level-test everyone: put them into their classes with an appropriate teacher. We have kids from three- to sixteen-years-old and we need to keep our eye on all of them all the time. When we go to the swimming pool in the afternoons we have to put everyone on buses to transport them the two kilometres to where the pool is located. This requires 'military precision'! Luckily, the team have become experts over the years though.

By far the most important aspect of my job is Health and Safety. That includes evaluation and assessment of the systems used in the workplace, and the things that worry me most – allergies. Imagine what could happen if a child who is allergic to nuts or fish forgets to wear their badge. Thankfully, the teaching staff and the kitchen staff all have a printed list, which includes photos, to check and double-check that those pupils are given the right food.

Finally, we can get down to teaching. Our school prides itself on its reputation. We try to give people an experience they'll want to tell their friends about, and we think we offer a good balance of academic work and other activities. The kids do art, music, drama – all in English. They have a talent show twice during the month. It's incredible to see the children doing tricks, singing songs and doing dance routines. We get so many talented people here. Sometimes, some of the children take over from the teachers and lead workshops. For example, last year there was a boy called Pedro who showed everyone some paper animals he had made, and then taught everyone how to make one of their own. My favourite activity, having been a sports monitor of course, is sports. We have an 'olympics' on the last day where we give prizes to all the participants. It's not the winning, it's the taking part that counts after all. Then, to finish with a bang we have a big water fight. The kids love it! I'm not sure the mums and dads do though!

[tone]

Part 3

Audio track: FCE_Listening_5_3.mp3

Now turn to Part 3. You hear five people talking about how they keep fit. For questions 19–23, assign the correct speaker to the statement given. There are three extra options which you do not have to use. You now have 30 seconds to look at Part 3.

[tone]

Speaker 1 I enjoy exercising, but it's true that I have followed some good advice to make it easier for myself. I exercise at the same time every day, 365 days a year. That's right - even at weekends. I only exercise for about 45 minutes each day, but I'm very strict about how I do it. So, I know what I'm going to do every day: two days in the pool, three days in the gym and two days of running. As long as I keep to my programme, it's easy.

Speaker 2 The thing is, I'm really slim and I feel really good, and I don't think that I need to exercise. So I just don't think it's necessary. I know there are many reasons to keep in shape such as needing to lose weight or having a health problem, but I don't have those issues. I watch what I eat and keep reasonably active. I'm perfect. I do do some exercise, but it's a real effort.

Speaker 3 I always found it difficult to go to the gym and just pump iron or do cardio by myself. I was always sporty when I was at school, but when I left I just stopped. For a while I couldn't figure out why that was. Then someone pointed out that it was because at school we always did team sports or things where we were in a group. Once I had established *that,* there was no problem and now I get together with friends to play soccer two nights a week and I go out with a running group on Sunday night.

Speaker 4 Obviously, exercising is important. A person who does sport will be healthier than a person who doesn't, I admit, but I really think a lot of what causes people to rush to the gym is fear. And some good marketing. Going to the gym is expensive. Everyone is told that you need to pay to join a gym, as well as buy all the branded sports shoes and clothes. And how many people pay for the gym every month, or for the whole year, just to make themselves feel better? Loads. In the future people will realise it's all just a bit of a fad.

Speaker 5 I exercise two or three times per week. I think it's really important to keep in shape. I love to go running in the morning and I'll go to the swimming pool from time to time. I don't have much of a routine, though. I just work out when I can. I also eat sensibly. I don't eat junk food or sweets much. That helps. I would love to join a gym, firstly because it would give me a better routine and, secondly, because it would be good to use the sauna and go to the classes and stuff. But it's just too pricey, and you generally need to sign up for about a year for one of those contracts.

Part 4

Audio track: FCE_Listening_5_4.mp3

Now turn to Part 4. You hear an interview with John, a successful barrister, talking about his career. For questions 24–30, choose the best answer, A, B or C. You will now have one minute to look at Part 4.

[tone]

Interviewer: Can we begin with you telling me how you became interested in a legal career?

John: Honestly, it was a mix of things. To start with, I was thinking about studying History at university. I was good at evaluating evidence and writing essays, so it seemed like a good fit for my skills. But luckily the careers teacher at school handed me a leaflet about careers in Law. One look at the salaries on offer to lawyers, and I was suddenly a lot less interested in History! There were other factors, like job security and flexibility and enjoying a good challenge, but the money was the biggest incentive at first.

Interviewer: So, did you enjoy your course at university? What was it like?

John: In a word: tough. Studying law is one long intellectual assault course. I still remember the shock of how difficult my first assignment was. The entire class stayed up all night to finish that essay! And it's not just about hitting the books to acquire all of the necessary knowledge of legislation. Even if you knew everything, you'd still have the challenge of using all of your analytical skills to arrive at the correct interpretation of the law. There's argument involved, too. You can rarely just say 'This is the answer'. You have to be able to justify your answer. Always.

Interviewer: And after university graduation, how did you begin your career?

John: Lawyers are fortunate. We belong to a profession that is committed to training and development, to recruiting the best and brightest to be the next generation of lawyers. By the time you graduate you already have the contacts and work experience you need to make getting a job a less daunting prospect. I'd recommend any aspiring lawyers to begin looking at the websites for law firms for opportunities to do work experience or internships. You can be building your knowledge of the business of law even before you graduate.

Interviewer: So now you're a barrister. Can you explain what that actually means?

John: Most people think I spend all my time in court, but that's very far from the truth. Basically, my job is to advise my clients on how best to resolve their legal issues – whatever they are. In many ways, if they get to court I haven't done my job properly. Most disputes should be settled without the need for the expense of trial. But if the case does come to trial, it's my job to represent my client and make sure the judge sees their side of the dispute properly.

Interviewer: So, if you're not in court all of the time, where are you?

John: Good question! I'm mainly in my office in the middle of London. If I'm not in conference with my clients, I'm usually at my desk ploughing through paperwork or catching up on the latest legislation. Sometimes I travel to different places around the UK to meet clients and witnesses. And from time to time I get to work from home. One drawback I should mention is the long hours. I get to work very early and leave very late, plus I often end up working at the weekend.

Interviewer: And what do you enjoy most about your job?

John: It's challenging and I get to meet lots of different people. But the best thing is learning every day about different areas of Law and of the world. One day I might be getting acquainted with the business of international shipping, the next day I'm talking to advertisers. The day after that it's plastics manufacturers. I have to get to the bottom of all these different industries so that I can understand my clients' problems. The money is good, but, now that I'm comfortable, it's not the main motivation.

[tone]

Transcripts

Test 6

Part 1

Audio track: FCE_Listening_6_1.mp3

FCE Academy, listening practice for the Cambridge English First FCE examination. As it is in the exam, each recording will be introduced and you will have time to read the questions before the recording is played. In the exam, you will hear each recording twice. At the beginning of each recording you will hear this sound: [tone]. It is good practice to write notes while you listen to each recording.

Part 1: You will hear people speaking in eight different situations. For questions 1–8, you must choose the best answer, A, B or C.

Question 1 You hear two customers talking in a hairdressing salon. What style does one recommend?

[tone]

Woman A: Morning. Have you been coming here for long?

Woman B: Morning. Yes, for at least ten years now. Sascha really gets my hair.

Woman A: I heard he was good. He did my friend's hair for her wedding and she was over the moon with it. It looked amazing.

Woman B: I'm sure it did. What are you having done today?

Woman A: I can't decide. I want to do something radical but I'm in two minds about it. I fancy a shorter cut.

Woman B: That will be a big change!

Woman A: I know! I've had long hair since I was at school. Definitely time for a change.

Woman B: Have you asked Sascha what he thinks?

Woman A: Yes. He says with curly hair like mine, a short cut can look really good.

Woman B: There you are then

[tone]

Question 2 You hear a woman talking about the time her son forgot her birthday. What does she say he did to apologise?

[tone]

I can't believe he did it again – every year it's the same story! Yes, he lives far away so it's out of the question, really, for him to come to visit, but he could have apologised. Not even a phone call, just a card saying 'Forgive Me' – again. It's all very well to beg forgiveness, but did he really mean it? I suppose he did send flowers, which made it up for it, and he's a good boy really. It's just nice to think someone cares.

[tone]

Question 3 You hear a mechanic talking to a customer. What's the problem with the car?

[tone]

It's still going strong, even if it is an antique, and you'll probably get another 20,000 kilometres out of it, but you need to address the current problem – it would be dangerous not to. In fact, if you don't change at least two of them you could get in serious trouble with the police. I know you only drive to and from work each day – just a few kilometres – and that's all fair and well, but the front left one is completely worn out! It will burst if you keep driving it like that. Please take my advice and have it replaced – soon!

[tone]

Question 4 You hear a nurse talking. Why did she become a nurse?

[tone]

I take after my mother in so many ways, and so it made complete sense for me to want to do something similar to what she did – she was a doctor, by the way. The idea of giving back to society and helping people in need is something very close to my heart, and I sleep well at night knowing I'm doing a good thing. It's a great job, and of course I need the money, but I'd probably do it for free, if I'm honest. Especially the work I'm doing right now on the children's ward. Those poor little people, so scared and confused. Helping them is what I've always wanted to do.

[tone]

Question 5 You hear a bus driver speaking about his job. What's the worst part of the job for him?

[tone]

I suppose I'd be crazy if I said I didn't like driving buses, having done it for 20 years now, and the pay's okay – not as bad as it used to be and good enough to make ends meet – and, yes, it can be lonely work, as you're on your own most of the time, but I do bump into other drivers at the station and we always have a laugh together. And my passengers are always friendly enough. It's the shifts that I can't put up with, especially not knowing what hours I'll be working from one day to the next.

[tone]

Question 6 You hear two historians speaking. What are they talking about?

[tone]

Man: ... and so that brings us on to the next era.

Woman: Yes, it was with the advent of farming that the first communities, as we might define them now, were established. We now know this to be the start of modern human history. The text books need to be rewritten.

Man: We know this was a period when they were settling down into larger groups, establishing and cultivating crops, allowing time to do other things with their time, like thinking.

Woman: ... and this was still thousands of years before any form of written record was developed.

Man: Yes, written in the sense we know it now at least. Hieroglyph or sanskrit were many years in the future, but we can find evidence of their settlements and activities from other sources ... (fade)

[tone]

Question 7 You hear Tom talking about his boss, Rich. What does he say about him?

[tone]

My boss Rich is a great guy – usually. He's always smiling in the office and always has a kind word to say about colleagues, but when it comes to my work it's a different matter completely. For example, I gave him a job I had done last week, which I thought was really good – actually it was almost the same as a piece of work he had approved the previous month – but this time he wrote a long list, detailing problems. He also gave me a warning and told me to improve my attitude. I'm now really worried about the next piece I hand in: who knows what he'll say?

[tone]

Question 8 You hear a woman talking about her wedding. Where is the wedding going to take place?

[tone]

I've been to so many weddings now – probably 20 or so – and, if I'm honest, I can't really remember anything special about any of them. One thing I am sure about though, now that I'm getting married myself, is that I want mine to be different. There'll be some traditional bits, like a big white dress and wedding vows, but the location will be far from what people would normally expect. I'm thinking white sand beaches and coconut trees and beautiful sunsets – somewhere that you couldn't say was not exotic! I reckon that's what will stick in people's minds for years to come, and that's something I think is really important. I'll have to let everyone know, with lots of time to make plans to travel, mind you.

[tone]

Part 2

Audio track: FCE_Listening_6_2.mp3

Now turn to Part 2. You hear Rob Baxendale talking about learning to play the cello at the age of 40. For questions 9–18, complete the sentences with a word or short phrase. You now have 45 seconds to look at Part 2.

[tone]

Interviewer: There's a real trend at the moment for people returning to music. Do you see yourself as part of a cultural phenomenon?

Rob: Maybe. I mean, I think it's a fairly common feeling when you get to a certain age: you realise that you've lost so much of the enthusiasm you had for hobbies and interests when you were younger – there's not much time for these things when you're bringing up kids or holding down a 9–5 job. So, maybe you were planning to carry on playing your instrument after leaving school, but then one day you realise it's been ten years since you got it out of its case.

Interviewer: So, what made you get out your cello again?

Rob: An old friend of mine is still a keen cellist, and we got talking about his orchestra, and how much he enjoys preparing for public performances. It reminded me of how much I used to love that, too. My daughter has been having violin lessons at school and last June I watched her make her first public solo performance – I was so proud. Spurred on by that I thought 'why shouldn't I learn with her?' I then drove back to my parents' home and got my cello out of my old bedroom. I think they were glad to see the back of it – it's massive!

Interviewer: So, tell me, how was it getting started again? Had you forgotten everything?

Rob: No, not really, but you do kind of have to start over. It's not just a matter of picking up where you left off, so, for me, it's been a 'back-to-basics' approach to make sure I'm not missing anything important. Obviously, I remember some things, but I'm amazed by how much I've forgotten.

Interviewer: So, you're playing along with your daughter now? What's that like?

Rob: My daughter has helped me to remember a lot of the simple folk tunes you tend to find in beginners' books, and I try to play with her when I can – it's great practice: nice and simple. But she's a much faster learner than me! One good thing about learning as an adult, for me, though, is that I'm much more aware of technique now. I don't think kids appreciate how important this is. I certainly didn't.

Interviewer: Yes, that can be a little boring, I suppose. Do you and your daughter have the same teacher then?

Rob: No, I mean I did ask – but the teacher said he only works with schools. It was actually pretty hard finding a teacher who would work with me. Cello teachers are thin on the ground – there simply aren't that many of them, especially as I live quite a long way from any large towns, but I eventually tracked someone down who was actually living just a few streets away. She's just moved up from London and was happy to look at giving me lessons in the evenings. We get on really well, actually, so that's a huge bonus.

Interviewer: Does she give you lots of homework?

Rob: You wouldn't believe how much! Practice is so important, but don't forget I'm still working full-time. I think I only manage around two hours a week.

Interviewer: That seems quite a lot to me.

Rob: You know that rule that says it takes ten thousand hours to become an expert in something? I worked out that it would take 48 years to get there at the rate I practise! That could be quite depressing if I wanted to be an international-standard cellist, but luckily my only ambition is to play with a smaller local orchestra - for fun.

Interviewer: So, what are you finding most difficult about the instrument this time? Are there any particular challenges?

Rob: Well, it's a little technical, which can be frustrating. I have most issues with fingering, and trying to get that right means I'm playing a lot more slowly than the composers intended. Also, I'm reading a lot of music theory, and that can get very complicated, but I think the main thing for me is learning to listen to the sound of the cello again. That's harder than you might think as you need to really concentrate.

[tone]

Part 3

Audio track: FCE_Listening_6_3.mp3

Now turn to Part 3. You hear five people talking about teachers from their school days. For questions 19–23, assign the correct speaker to the statement given. There are three extra options which you do not have to use. You now have 30 seconds to look at Part 3.

[tone]

Speaker 1 Everyone remembers a particular teacher from school, don't they? Unfortunately, I remember one for all the wrong reasons. Mr Morris was my Math teacher and he was really horrible to me. I mean, really horrible. I was never good at that subject and Mr Morris used to single me out in class all the time. I used to be so scared of him I would shake before going into Math class. Even if I got the answer right he would clap sarcastically. He was just plain nasty to me.

Speaker 2 When I was at school I found it hard to really get involved with the work. Some people would say I was uncooperative – others might think I just wasn't very clever. That was until I met Mr May. He set an example I will never forget: he was well-organised, well-informed and, to top it all, he had a natural ability to transmit that knowledge to his students. Still, to this day, whenever I have a problem, I ask myself: 'What would Mr May do?'

Speaker 3 Mrs Garcia was the teacher that all the boys fancied. She was Spanish and was very beautiful and exotic to us all – she had this wonderful accent and seemed younger than all the other teachers, and more fun, too. Maybe she was younger. Anyway, the problem was, any time she wanted me to speak I was just too shy and couldn't get a word out. I went bright red every single time she spoke to me for the entire time I was in her class. But I wasn't the only one: it was a popular class. Strangely enough, more people opted for Spanish in those years than ever before. Mostly boys, of course!

Speaker 4 Mrs Brown was always my favourite teacher. In these days of equality and, dare I say, feminism, it's easy for young women to receive mixed messages and be unclear about their role in society. She was a Home Economics teacher and she taught me how to do many practical things that are necessary to know. Yes, she taught cooking and things like sewing and knitting, but she didn't tell us that these things were only for women. She insisted that the boys all learned these things, too. Quite right. She was all about equality, but also knew the importance of taking pride in your home and family. As I say: my favourite teacher.

Speaker 5   Mr Simpson was a Maths teacher I had when I was about 11. He brought Maths to life because he would teach it in a real-life context. So. he'd teach you why it was important to be able to do long division, or give you a scenario of building a house and show you why knowing trigonometry was so essential. Mr Simpson actually reminds me of several bosses I have had over the years: he never put up with any nonsense, but he was always polite and professional. I think his style of teaching set me up for life and taught me so many important things.

Part 4

Audio track: FCE_Listening_6_4.mp3

Now turn to Part 4. You hear an interview with a woman called Sarah Mortimer, a body painter. For questions 24–30, choose the best answer, A, B or C. You will now have one minute to look at Part 4.

[tone]

Interviewer: Welcome, everyone. We're joined today by Sarah Mortimer, who's here to talk to us about body painting. So, Sarah, how did you end up doing this for a living?

Sarah: Thank you. Okay. So, I've always been interested in Art, and while I was at school I watched a documentary on face painting and I suppose I must have remembered something about it from then. But it wasn't until much later, when I was studying for my degree in Art, that I did it for the first time. My sister asked me if I could do some face painting at my nephew's birthday party.

Interviewer: Ah! A family connection. And how did it develop from there?

Sarah: Well, that party started it all, actually. One of my sister's friends liked what I was doing and asked me to come to her child's party the next week, and this time I'd get paid for it! Doing something so fun, and which made other people so happy, would always have been attractive to me. However, getting some reimbursement for my efforts and using that income to put myself through college was the incentive to continue. But, while that might have been the motivation I needed to get started, it definitely isn't the reason I've continued.

Interviewer: Okay. Kids' parties are one thing, but you're now at a whole different level. When did you start taking body painting seriously in its own right?

Sarah: I suppose that after doing a degree in Fine Art most people would expect me to become a classroom teacher, or maybe a poor artist, but when I picked up a magazine that contained a piece about the body painting movement I realised other people were doing it, too, and I decided to make a go of it – why not? My boyfriend joked about me becoming a clown – he's 'hilarious' – but I wasn't amused. These people in the magazine were doing it in a very expressive way: they were serious artists. Sure, they might still be doing the kids' parties to earn some cash, but what they were doing was more like serious tattoo artistry than just face painting.

Interviewer: I see. So, I guess, soon after that you got the chance to work with some of the top names in the business. Tell us about that.

Sarah: Okay. So. I started attending some workshops with more experienced body painters all over the country and I actually won a prize for one of my pieces. That resulted in a masterclass with one of the top artists in the world at the time.

Interviewer: Ah, yes. Noel Fitzgibbon: what an interesting man! What do you think made you so successful so early?

Sarah: Well, I really made an impression with my painting ability, I think – something I suppose I developed on the university course – and I approached that course very seriously: I was focused on making it a success. And I met some really well-known practitioners there, too, and the whole experience unexpectedly opened the world of body painting up to me.

Interviewer: Your career has recently taken another very interesting turn when you got involved in Art Therapy. What can you tell us about that?

Sarah: Yes. It was actually during a coffee break on the course that I first discovered body painting Art Therapy. One of the tutors was saying that it can be used in hospitals to cheer people up and to allow them to express themselves, and that it was becoming an accepted treatment in the field of mental health. I hadn't thought about it before, it just seemed obvious all of a sudden that this was what I wanted to do – giving something back to people who need it. So, I studied for a Masters in Art Therapy and the rest is history.

[tone]

Transcripts   Test 7

Part 1

Audio track: FCE_Listening_7_1.mp3

FCE Academy, listening practice for the Cambridge English First FCE examination. As it is in the exam, each recording will be introduced and you will have time to read the questions before the recording is played. In the exam, you will hear each recording twice. At the beginning of each recording you will hear this sound: [tone]. It is good practice to write notes while you listen to each recording.

Part 1: You will hear people speaking in eight different situations. For questions 1–8, you must choose the best answer, A, B or C.

Question 1 You hear two writers speaking about a piece of work. How do they feel?

[tone]

Man: Well, it's been a lot of late nights and long weekends, but we're definitely getting there.

Woman: So, what do you think of our progress so far?

Man: I'm a little worried, actually. I know you're never 100% happy with your own work but I expected to feel a greater sense of satisfaction at this point than I do.

Woman: What concerns me is that we've done all this work and we aren't really sure if anyone is going to like it! It would just be disappointing if we had to start all over again.

Man: Well, let's hope that isn't going to happen.

Woman: OK. Let's pause, review what we've done and then decide where to go from here. What do you think?

Man: OK. Good plan.

[tone]

Question 2 You hear a swimmer talking about her career. What does she think she would like to do next?

[tone]

Right after the world championships I decided enough was enough and it was time to retire from competition. Some people decide to do something completely different, away from sport, but I've never even considered that. Swimming has been my life since I was a child and doing anything other than sport would be unthinkable. I was lucky enough to finish right at the top and because of that I knew lots of journalists and presenters from TV and radio, and I think I'd like to follow that career path. Commentating on and writing about the sports I love would be a dream come true.

[tone]

Question 3   You hear a man calling his gym about a class. Why is he calling?

[tone]

Hi, can I speak to the manager please? Oh, good. Yes – I wanted to speak to you about doing a course or a class or something ... I'll tell you what the problem is: I have a young child who is full of energy. I'm an older parent and I'm afraid I just can't keep up with him. I need to do something because it's starting to get me down. I wonder if I could come in to meet you – maybe you could give me some advice on where to start?

[tone]

Question 4   You hear two friends speaking about an app. What do they agree on?

[tone]

Woman: So, you just download it straight to your phone and follow the instructions. It's really simple to use.
Man: Not for me. Maybe it's just my phone, but some of the features are ridiculously complicated. It would be really handy if I could get it to work, though.
Woman: It is handy. I use it all the time.
Man: To be honest, I wouldn't want to. Who wants to share their pictures and tell their friends what they're doing every five minutes? It'll never catch on.

[tone]

Question 5   You hear a man talking about his job. How does he feel?

[tone]

I couldn't wait to get started when I got the job. I had all these great ideas and plans to revolutionise the design process in the office, but my new boss just kind of looked at me like I was from another planet – with total confusion when I tried to explain my vision to him. I thought when you become a manager you'd have the freedom to try new things and make an impact, but that just isn't the case in this company. It's all people-management, admin and meetings. It's so dull. If I could go back to my old job, I would. It was much more interesting and far more creative.

[tone]

Question 6   You hear a woman talking on the phone about an order she has made. What does she say?

[tone]

Yes, that's right. I've been waiting all morning and it still hasn't come ... No, don't cancel it! That's out of the question. I simply want it put off until tomorrow ... It can? Great! But will it definitely come tomorrow before 2? I need to be at work by 3 every day – I really should have explained that in the first place. So, if you can contact the driver and tell him not to come that would be perfect. OK. Have a good day. Thank you.

[tone]

Question 7   You hear a taxi driver talking to a passenger. What can't the passenger do?

[tone]

Taxi driver: Here we are – Apple Tree Drive. Number 7, wasn't it?
Passenger: That's right. Thanks driver. How much is it?
Taxi driver: £15.40, sir. So how long are you staying for?
Passenger: Oh, just for the weekend, unfortunately. It looks such a great city! ... Oh no! I'm afraid I don't have any cash. I'll need to get you to put it on my card. Is that okay?
Taxi driver: I'm sorry mate, but my card machine's out of order. It says so on the

sign here – look.

Passenger: Ah, yes. I didn't see that when I got in. Sorry. Tell you what, just let me go into the hotel and explain the problem. I'm sure I can pick up enough from Reception to cover it and they can add it to my bill. I can leave them my card as a guarantee.

Taxi driver: That sounds fair enough. I'll wait here for you, but try to be quick – I shouldn't be parked here!

[tone]

Question 8   You hear two people talking in a supermarket. What do they agree on?

[tone]

Man: I admit – it's not the place if you want to pick up bargains, but you get what you pay for.

Woman: Maybe. But I just don't know if it's worth the extra that you pay.

Man: Where else can you go shopping at midnight around here? And the variety of goods they have makes it worth the extra, I'd say.

Woman: They do have exceptional choice. I can't argue with that. The best, in fact, but it's still too expensive.

[tone]

Part 2

Audio track: FCE_Listening_7_2.mp3

Now turn to Part 2. You hear Duncan, a keen surfer from Sydney in Australia. For questions 9–18, complete the sentences with a word or short phrase. You now have 45 seconds to look at Part 2.

[tone]

Whenever I meet people from outside Australia, I find they have a certain picture of what Aussies are like. They think we all have barbecues on the beach every day, or drive round the Outback in trucks dodging kangaroos. In reality, most Australians live completely ordinary lives that are no different to people in Europe or the US. However, there is one stereotype which I'm happy to live up to: I'm a real Australian surfer.

Living in Sydney means that I'm only a few miles away from one of the best surfing beaches in Australia: Manly Beach. The more famous Bondi Beach tends to be more crowded, so I've always preferred Manly. It's a long beach with good breaks – waves – all along its length. On Saturdays I can just take a ferry across the harbour and I'm there. I started going to Manly with my dad, when I was 7 or 8, and I took lessons every weekend. There are still plenty of surf schools there. You'll usually find me at the north end of the beach, which offers more excitement, although I wouldn't recommend it to an inexperienced surfer.

But I would recommend going to a school rather than learning on your own. They can teach you how to surf safely and how to behave around other surfers. For example, the first surfer to reach a wave has priority – that's an unofficial rule – you have to leave them to it and catch the next one. And a good teacher will tell you when to ditch your board and when to hang on to it. Unless you're going to wipe-out, you should always keep hold of your board: abandoned boards can seriously injure other surfers. For a few dollars a week, you can learn a hobby that will last you the rest of your life, and hopefully you'll avoid any serious mishaps as you enjoy yourself.

Probably the most dangerous aspect of the sea to a beginner are the rip tides. That's why it's never a good idea to surf on a new beach without consulting a local expert. A rip tide is a strong current that heads out to sea, and you can find yourself dragged along with it before you know what's happening. The best advice is to paddle sideways across the rip, rather than trying to swim against it. But the biggest danger to an inexperienced surfer is themself: learners can find themselves in unfamiliar waters, making mistakes that can lead to nasty bumps and scrapes, or even find themselves so far out to sea that they can't swim back to shore. You shouldn't really begin surfing unless you're fairly physically fit.

Of course, surfing isn't all about the action. There are quieter parts to the hobby, too.

A lot of surfers enjoy the simple process of waxing their surfboards. First of all, you have to scrape off all the old wax using a special wax comb – I find washing-up liquid helps – then you have to apply a base coat of new wax, which needs to be bumpy so that it can take the top coat. Different surfers have different approaches to this: some go in circles, some in zigzag lines. And finally there's the top coat of wax. You have to choose the right kind: the wax for warmer waters, like in Australia, is different to the wax you might want to use in Europe.

All in all, surfing is a great way to spend your free time. It's a hobby that takes you outside rather than sitting watching TV – it's great exercise, and it's relatively cheap. I'm proud to be an Aussie surfer.

[tone]

Part 3

Audio track: FCE_Listening_7_3.mp3

Now turn to Part 3. You hear five people talking about their experience of working at a holiday resort. For questions 19–23, assign the correct speaker to the statement given. There are three extra options which you do not have to use. You now have 30 seconds to look at Part 3.

[tone]

Speaker 1 Fort Happy is a traditional holiday destination for everyone – generally people with children – people who need to relax and be entertained. It pays to be happy and cheerful if you want a job in a place like this. Generally, people want positive people around when they're on a holiday. And that suits me! And I'm happy to do whatever job I'm asked to. One minute I'm serving tables, the next I'm doing a kid's party. I just love how it's always different.

Speaker 2 You could look at it as a really negative thing, but I don't – I've actually worked here for the past two summers and hope to again in the coming year. Thing is, they never have enough staff, which means you're always run off your feet. But that also means there's loads of overtime every month, and, when you're so busy working, time passes really quickly. I'm a student and the extra cash really comes in handy during the year. Okay, so when I finish studying it's not really what I want to be doing, but for now it's perfect. I'm much better off than any of my friends.

Speaker 3 I perform eight times a week here: twice on a Saturday and Sunday, and then four other days. It's hard work, but then that's show business. It's a long way to the top, as they say. I've been performing at Camp Happy for the last two seasons now, and I've really benefited from being able to perform my act over and over again. Because of that, I feel I have what it takes to get to the next level. All the big artists started like this.

Speaker 4 I've always enjoyed the work but never got on with the Entertainments Manager. I've already handed in my notice, in fact: I won't be back. But I must say, for some people, working with the public is the ideal job. I think I'd tell anyone to try it out because it's so much fun, and changing jobs each day was always interesting for me – I got to try out loads of different things. But I've just grown up and grown out of it I think, though, and it's time to go.

Speaker 5 It's great to work with people who are on holiday and having a good time, but the problem is I just want to join them on holiday and not do any work. I'd much rather be the served rather than the server, but maybe everyone feels that way. And I dream of meeting my Mr Right here – he'll say to me 'take off those waitress clothes and join me by the pool', and we'll live happily ever after. I'm just so fed up here. I'd rather do just about anything other than this.

Part 4

Audio track: FCE_Listening_7_4.mp3

Now turn to Part 4. You hear an interview with Dave Willis, a teacher at an international school in Malaysia. For questions 24–30, choose the best answer, A, B or C. You will now have one minute to look at Part 4.

[tone]

Interviewer: Hi Dave. So, you began your teaching career in the UK. What was that like?

Dave: Hi John. Like a lot of teachers in the UK, I became very dissatisfied with my job early on. Most teachers start out as idealists who think they'll be changing children's lives. What happens in the UK is that you spend half your life doing paperwork – and I don't mean planning lessons, which is a part of the job I love: I'm perfectly at home on a Sunday searching the internet for exactly the right resource for a lesson the next day. No, the paperwork that keeps British teachers working late is marking assessments and entering data into spreadsheets. It's all to do with monitoring and reporting on your class's progress, but it doesn't really benefit the children at all. If the politicians and those who set these ridiculous requirements listened more to the people who actually teach, the whole system would be in better shape, and fewer teachers would leave the profession. The pay, after all, is rather good.

Interviewer: Is that – all the paperwork – what made you think about teaching outside the UK?

Dave: That, plus I've always had itchy feet. I travelled a bit as a student and I fell in love with the feeling of adventure: of being somewhere that isn't 'boring old England'. Somewhere there's a good chance of sunshine every day! And, once I began looking at the adverts for international schools, I realised there was great potential for someone like me. There are schools teaching in English in almost every city of the world, and they're crying out for teachers who qualified in the UK. I've taught in Spain, Egypt, and now Malaysia.

Interviewer: What was it like, moving so far away?

Dave: Well, I was young at the time – still only in my late twenties – and I didn't have many ties to the UK. It wasn't quite as simple as packing my bag and jumping on a plane, though, but actually it was pretty easy. I did a few job interviews on Skype before settling on a school in Spain that looked interesting, and where they needed someone with my experience. Because Spain isn't far from the UK I was able to make a few weekend trips to find myself an apartment and get to know the area before starting. The biggest headache in Spain, though, is all the administration you have to do just to be able to work there – I spent ages in the lobbies of government buildings getting my paperwork sorted out.

Interviewer: What's different about international schools?

Dave: Everybody asks me that – especially teachers back home! One big difference is the parents. In general, they're far more engaged with their children's education than parents in the UK are. Of course, I'm generalising here. Naturally, all parents want the best for their children, but, in international schools, this means they keep a very close eye on the teacher, and have very high expectations of academic success. That has good sides and bad sides from the teacher's point of view: parents tend to be competitive, and this can lead to complaints if their child is not doing as well as their friends, and so a lot of my job is keeping parents happy. Fortunately, though, they seem to like my approach and appreciate my results.

Interviewer: Have you had to adjust your style of teaching in any way?

Dave: Not especially. In fact, in most of the places I've taught, my job has been to make the teaching style *more* like that of the UK. Traditionally, a lot of international schools use the 'chalk and talk' approach, where the teacher is more like a lecturer, standing at the front and delivering the lesson to the class. The students just sit there quietly and take notes. But more forward-looking schools want to encourage children to be active learners, which means a lot more talk in the classroom, more projects, and more creativity. It can look and sound very different to the more traditional teachers.

Interviewer: Do you think you'll ever go back to the UK?

Dave: That's a tricky question. On the one hand I've begun to put down roots here in Malaysia: I have children of my own who are at school here, and I wouldn't be too keen on changing their lives so dramatically. Not now, anyway. And we have a great apartment and a good, healthy lifestyle, with an active expat community. And I love teaching here. But, on the other hand, I'm not sure I'd want to retire here and never live in England again. I think I might want to return home when I get a little older. Fortunately, that decision is a few years off.

[tone]

Transcripts   Test 8

Part 1

Audio track: FCE_Listening_8_1.mp3

FCE Academy, listening practice for the Cambridge English First FCE examination. As it is in the exam, each recording will be introduced and you will have time to read the questions before the recording is played. In the exam, you will hear each recording twice. At the beginning of each recording you will hear this sound: [tone]. It is good practice to write notes while you listen to each recording.

Part 1: You will hear people speaking in eight different situations. For questions 1–8, you must choose the best answer, A, B or C.

Question 1   You hear a woman talking about her weekend. What did she do?

[tone]

Well, we try to do it at least a couple of times a year – it depends very much on the weather, of course: we invite our friends and there's usually a party of about eight of us. We pack up all our equipment – remembering the badminton racquets and football, of course – then it's off to wherever we fancy. It's best to use a proper site, though, one which will have hot water and electricity, but just being out in the open air is simply amazing for me. The kids love it, of course, and so do my husband and I.

[tone]

Question 2   You hear a man describing yesterday's meeting. How did his boss behave?

[tone]

Okay. So, I think he has good intentions – he does it every time actually. Right. So, we were in the meeting and half-way through discussing the planning stage of the project, and everyone thought we were on the right track. Then he came out with all these issues and things that he demanded be changed. There was no negotiation: with him it's just, 'Do it this way - because I said so.' He's confrontational and a bit of a bully, actually, and no-one likes that. I think he really needs to give more credit to the professionals on the team.

[tone]

Question 3   You hear two people discussing the weather. How is the weather going to be tomorrow, according to the forecast?

[tone]

Woman: So, looks like it's going to brighten up at last!

Man: I hope it does – I'm sick of this constant rain. It's been like this for weeks!

Woman: Yes, I know but I've seen on two different weather reports that we're over that now. I might even go to the park tomorrow to see if I can get a tan. Would you like to come along?

Man: Let's see what happens. I remember once last year they forecasted a sunny day and I woke up to snow on the ground! And it didn't stop snowing for a week!

[tone]

Question 4 You hear two students talking. What is the problem?

[tone]

Tom: Hi Rosie. Looks like you had the same problem as me then.

Rosie: Hi Tom. Yeah, is it the Number 36 you get?

Tom: Usually – but today it just didn't turn up.

Rosie: How long did you wait then?

Tom: Not too long. After 10 minutes I looked online and it said there was a problem on the High Street, so I know no buses would be coming – so I just walked round to the train station. It's the longer way, but I'm here now.

Rosie: I wish I'd done that. I waited for 30 minutes and then had to jump in a taxi. Cost a fortune, too!

[tone]

Question 5 You hear two people talking about the music they are listening to. What does the woman say about the music playing?

[tone]

Man: Oh, listen – I love this song. Is it Kil Follins?

Woman: Yes, it is. I love it, too. I remember when it came out. I must have been 15.

Man: Me too! It makes me remember Jessica, my girlfriend at the time.

Woman: Really? It always makes me want to cry. Do you remember the video?

Man: Oh yeah, that's right – so depressing, but Jessica loved it. I wonder what she's up to these days.

[tone]

Question 6 You hear a woman talking about a crime series on TV. What does she say about the storylines?

[tone]

There are some great twists and turns, I'll give you that, but that in itself can get rather tedious. Do you know what I mean? He always does the same thing: just as he's leaving an interview with a suspect, he'll say something like, 'Just one last thing...' and then ask a cunning question that cracks the case wide open! It's great, but, for me, I just think it's just too far-fetched. You can't really enjoy it completely because the scenarios just don't seem that credible.

[tone]

Question 7 You hear a man speaking on a telephone. What is he trying to do?

[tone]

Hello. I have been having trouble with your self-service ticket machine. I put in my dates of travel and ordered a single ticket to the city centre, but then the screen went blank. I tried again and the same thing happened. I need to get to my hotel where I'm meeting some friends. Is there anything you can do to help me? There is nobody here in the station to talk to and I have to get the next one or else I'll be late.

[tone]

Question 8   You hear a doctor talk to a patient about their injury. What does the doctor advise them to do?

[tone]

Doctor: And how long has it been like this?

Patient: Well, about six weeks? I've started swimming instead of going the gym because I thought it would be easier on my body, but it doesn't seem to be helping. I'm in more pain now that I was before.

Doctor: It's true that swimming is one of the best forms of exercise, but if you are injured – like you are – it's just not going to make the problem better. What you need is complete rest – I think at least two weeks.

Patient: I thought stopping completely might just make the pain stop temporarily.

Doctor: No. What you need to do is start exercising again – gently – after the rest period. Swimming would be a good reintroduction – again, gradually do it, so we can monitor your recovery properly.

[tone]

Part 2

Audio track: FCE_Listening_8_2.mp3

Now turn to Part 2. You hear Jerome Lightyear talking about his career about a professional airline pilot. For questions 9–18, complete the sentences with a word or short phrase. You now have 45 seconds to look at Part 2.

[tone]

Well, first of all, it costs a lot of money to become a pilot in the UK. I mean, a lot. You need your ATPL, which is the Airline Transport Pilot's Licence, and that costs around fifty thousand pounds once you've done all the training. If you do it full-time, you can be qualified in eighteen months, but I was lucky enough to have an apprenticeship with British Airways and they paid for all of my training. It took me two years and I've been flying for them ever since – I've flown nearly 10,000 hours now, and have been to 156 countries (and counting). It's the best job in the world.

You don't need to have a university degree to become a pilot, but you do need to have good school grades in subjects like Maths, English and Science, and having a second language is definitely a bonus. I'm half French, so this really gave me an advantage early on. You also need to pass security checks, and that can take a while. They're really careful about who gets a licence, which is a good thing! And I remember there were several people on my course who didn't pass: they just didn't have what it takes, I suppose. Some of them were paying for it themselves, too. What a waste of money!

And there's a lot of study involved, and that's before you even step foot inside a cockpit. You could be the best student, get the best grades and then fail the simulator module of the exam. I guess the thought of putting someone's life at risk is pretty scary once you're sat behind the controls, but it actually has nothing to do with fear, if you ask me: You don't think of the passengers when you're getting ready for take-off – you have too much to think about! By the time you've got your first flight as captain, you'll have flown as co-pilot for at least 1,500 hours, so you know what you're doing. For a short flight, like from Heathrow to Madrid, there isn't even time to go to the toilet. You're working non-stop the whole way. It's only when you've landed and someone opens the door of the cockpit that you remember there are a couple of hundred passengers on board!

I've been flying professionally for ten years now, and I've come to the conclusion that pilots are strange people. They have to be. When you're flying a commercial airliner, like a 747, you have a great responsibility. It's very intense work and your brain releases a lot of adrenaline during each flight. But then, after you've landed safely and gone through airport security, you're soon on your own in a quiet hotel room and it feels lonely. You could be anywhere in the world, but after a while the hotel rooms start to look the same. But then, the next day, you're back in the cockpit, doing it all again. And that's what I love about it. Knowing that every flight will be different, and that you're good at what you do. But travelling all the time definitely puts pressure on your relationships, for sure. Many of my colleagues have been through divorces, actually. It's a shame. Luckily, I have a very understanding wife who I spend a lot of time with when I'm home. She works in Air Traffic Control, as it happens!

[tone]

Part 3

Audio track: FCE_Listening_8_3.mp3

Now turn to Part 3. You hear five people talking about their hobbies and interests. For questions 19–23, assign the correct speaker to the statement given. There are three extra options which you do not have to use. You now have 30 seconds to look at Part 3.

[tone]

Speaker 1   I love running around crazily on the field – even when I was younger I wasn't very good at it, but I've always just loved the game. I'm a doctor and I wouldn't say I ever disconnect completely, but it certainly helps me to calm down and therefore to deal with an otherwise stressful career. I get to see old friends, too, some of whom I went to school with. Ultimately, for me, it's the perfect way to chill.

Speaker 2   When I'm painting I have the ability to drift off into this kind of meditative state. And I take it quite seriously: I try my best to really express myself through my paintings, and I sometimes make presents of them for friends – once I even sold one! I think, if I hadn't become a lawyer, I'd have been a painter, professionally I mean. If only I could earn a living from it! Law is such a dreadfully stressful profession – even though I like it – but when I'm painting, I can just forget about it all – completely – for a little while, anyway.

Speaker 3   I think that the key to staying young is to keep active, both mentally and physically. So, I go to the gym, which, frankly, I find tortuous for the body, and also to Night School, where the classes give me a routine. I just need to keep learning. And History is a subject where you need to remember things – dates, names and so on – so it's good exercise for the brain, and mine really needs a work out! It's definitely the best way for strengthening the mind, and going to Night School allows me to do that.

Speaker 4   I love hill-walking and I go at least twice a month with a group of friends. I've been up the highest peak in the country, actually, so maybe it would sound more impressive if I said I loved mountain climbing! Whatever you call it, I do it to keep in shape. It's much more interesting than the gym, and I've never really been an 'athlete'. We set off early in the morning with sandwiches and a flask of something hot, walk for an hour or two and then have a nice rest. Then, off we go again. It's relaxed, but I'll tell you what: you'll sleep well after one of our treks.

Speaker 5   I study French twice a week at Night School and I go to a language exchange at least one other night – there are lots to choose from here. I'm quite good at it now, actually. Don't get me wrong, I do like French, but to tell the truth I just like meeting people. I try to practise with my husband at home, but, really, I just annoy him. He's actually French, you see, and isn't the most patient person in the world! Not with me, anyway. Maybe he doesn't think I'm doing a very good job of it, I don't know, but he's glad I can now communicate properly when we go to visit his family!

Part 4

Audio track: FCE_Listening_8_4.mp3

Now turn to Part 4. You hear an interview with Ray Portman, who has written a book called *Walking El Camino*. For questions 24–30, choose the best answer, A, B or C. You will now have one minute to look at Part 4.

[tone]

Interviewer: Hi Ray. Thanks for coming in. I loved the book *Walking el Camino*, by the way. You've inspired me, and I'm curious: you say that the experience changed your life. What exactly do you mean by that?

Ray: Well, walking *el Camino de Santiago* is an extremely personal thing to do. You walk alone, most of the time, and you think and think and think. After a while, you start to learn things about who you are. Things you wouldn't normally think about. After four weeks of this, I was a different person.

Interviewer: A happier person?

Ray: Yes. Definitely happier. With a different way of seeing the world.

Interviewer: What made you want to do it?

Ray: I came up with the idea after I split up with my girlfriend. I needed a big change in my life and I had heard about this spiritual walk across Spain from friends. I had some holiday to take from work and it just kind of worked out. Before I knew it, I was on a plane to France, where my walk would begin.

Interviewer: I thought it was a Spanish walk?

Ray: No. The walk ends in Santiago, in Spain, but it can be started from almost anywhere in the world. I took what's known as 'The French Way', starting on the French side of the Pyrenees and entering Spain from the north. That way is around 700 kilometers and takes around 35 days.

Interviewer: That's a lot of walking!

Ray: Yes it is! And the mountains are difficult, especially if there's snow, but after that the terrain is quite smooth. It takes a week to get used to it and find your pace.

Interviewer: Where did you sleep at night?

Ray: All along the route there are hostels dedicated to people walking the Camino. This is basic accommodation: a bed, a shower and breakfast. But that's all you need after a day's walking. You also get to meet very interesting people in these places. Everyone has their own reason for doing the walk you see.

Interviewer: What kind of people did you meet?

Ray: All kinds. And all ages. People in their seventies, younger people walking with friends, teenagers having a walking holiday. There's no normal type of person. Anyone and everyone can do it.

Interviewer: Did you ever want to give up, and go to a nice hotel? Maybe go to the beach?

Ray: Actually, I did find it hard at times. Especially when I'd been walking for hours without seeing another person. I got a bit lonely on those days, but I kept going. I was determined to finish it.

Interviewer: And what was it like when you finally did finish it? Was it how you expected it to be?

Ray: I knew that arriving in Santiago de Compostela and seeing the cathedral after walking so many kilometres could be an emotional experience. I must admit that I did cry. I don't know why. Lots of people do at that point, apparently. For me, I was just overcome by emotion. It was a very strange feeling because I'd become so used to walking every day, lost in my thoughts, that, when I finally reached the end, I realised that I wasn't prepared for it. I didn't want to stop, but at the same time I was glad to stop. I know that probably doesn't make much sense!

Interviewer: It does make sense. An emotional scene! If you could give advice to someone thinking about doing the *Camino* themselves, what would it be?

Ray: Do it. Just do it. I can't describe how good it is. All I can say is that it changed my life for the better. I feel that I can deal with anything now. I feel complete. Oh, yes: and invest in good shoes! You'll need them!

Interviewer: It's a wonderful story, Ray, and your book is a really interesting read. Thank you.

Ray: You're welcome.

[tone]

Transcripts   Test 9

Part 1

Audio track: FCE_Listening_9_1.mp3

FCE Academy, listening practice for the Cambridge English First FCE examination. As it is in the exam, each recording will be introduced and you will have time to read the questions before the recording is played. In the exam, you will hear each recording twice. At the beginning of each recording you will hear this sound: [tone]. It is good practice to write notes while you listen to each recording.

Part 1: You will hear people speaking in eight different situations. For questions 1–8, you must choose the best answer, A, B or C.

Question 1 You hear a careers consultant describing a teacher's job to some students. What drawback does she warn of?

[tone]

Teaching is a wonderful profession, but if you get into it you should do so having considered all the pros and cons. I used to be a teacher and my favourite thing was the planning: I loved finding just the right resource for my class and then seeing how it worked in the lesson. You have great holidays, it's true, and that's great to really relax and take a little time away from it all, but you'll need to put in a lot of extra hours and you rarely get to switch off completely during term time. I hated the administration that went with it, though. You spend hours marking and then need to spend hours more entering data into spreadsheets. Teachers give up a lot of their holidays and weekends to spend time on school-related activities. So, if you're not prepared for that, don't go into teaching.

[tone]

Question 2 You hear a man talking about a place he used to visit as a child. What point is he making?

[tone]

When I was a kid I never went on a foreign holiday – I didn't even get on a plane until I was about 18. We had a caravan by the English coast – well, it was my grandparents' actually, but all the family would go there to visit and my cousins and I would go off on adventures in the forest, or play football, or go to the beach. We used our imagination and we had fun from morning 'til night. The point I'm making is kids just need to let their hair down and enjoy themselves. If they can do that, they're happy. Many children expect to go on super-expensive foreign holidays to Europe or America these days, but those holidays are often less fun for kids.

[tone]

Question 3 You hear a police officer taking details of an incident from a member of the public. What crime is being reported?

[tone]

Police officer: Okay, sir – if you would start from the beginning...

Man: So, as I was saying, they just hang about outside my shop making a terrible noise. They scare my customers.

Police officer: We can't stop the boys and girls from gathering there: it's a public space and also their school is right across the road, so I'm afraid we can't really do anything about it, unless a crime has been committed.

Man: Well, officer, I believe it has. You see, two boys came in here earlier and I saw them shoplifting.

Police officer: Right, well that's a completely different matter then, sir. I can certainly do something about that. Can you identify these boys?

Man: Yes. We have a CCTV camera and I think that has captured everything.

[tone]

Question 4   You hear a kitchen salesman speaking with a customer. Why is his shop better than the competition?

[tone]

No. I'm sorry, we don't have it in red. Actually, no-one has ever asked for it in red before, but I can order it in. It's true we don't have as many options as they have next door, but our kitchens are the absolute best on the market: those mass-produced items don't even come close, even if they do come in all colours. We'll custom-build your kitchen, and it'll be guaranteed for 10 years, although I'm sure you'll never need it. Our competition just can't compete with that.

[tone]

Question 5   You hear a man speaking with his friend on the phone. Why won't he be going on the trip with his friend?

[tone]

It does sound like a great deal ... all-inclusive you say. That's superb .... Me? Phhhh! No, no way. I wish. I just can't afford it ... Well, not at the moment, anyway ... Yes, I know it's cheap but if I don't have it I just can't ... Well, that's what happens when you're unemployed ... Maybe next year?

[tone]

Question 6   You hear two women arranging a journey. What do they agree on?

[tone]

Woman A: But when you drive it really makes me feel sick: you're definitely the worst driver! I can drive if you like.

Woman B: Well, probably not, actually. My car, my rules. You always drive too fast, anyway.

Woman A: We want to get there quickly, don't we?

Woman B: My priority is getting there safely. Also, let's enjoy the scenery: it's lovely down there. When do you need to get back?

Woman A: I could do with getting back early Sunday afternoon, if possible. I need to get organised for Monday.

Woman B: That's perfect for me, too. I'm off Monday but I'd like to be home for Sunday evening.

[tone]

Question 7   You hear a woman asking for advice from a pharmacist. What does the pharmacist say the woman must do?

[tone]

Woman: Hello. I wonder if you could help me? I've got a terribly sore throat – I've suffered from tonsillitis in the past and think maybe I have it again.

Pharmacist: Let me have a look – Yes, I think it could well be.

Woman: Can you give me some medicine for it? The doctor's surgery is closed now until Monday.

Pharmacist: I can give you something, but what you need is penicillin, and I can't give you that without a prescription from your doctor.

Woman: And is that the same for all pharmacies? Are there not pharmacists who can write a prescription?

Pharmacist: I'm afraid not. I can give you these sweets and some paracetamol, but not the antibiotics you need, I'm afraid. Sorry.

[tone]

Question 8 You hear a physicist talking about playing the violin. What does he say about it?

[tone]

When I've been studying a lot, I love nothing more than picking up my instrument and having a play. I study that, too, I suppose, and I love to find patterns in the music – I approach each piece like it's a puzzle to be solved. In that way, I guess it's a bit like science. There's usually a solution, although in both science and music I must say I'm often lost for the answer, but the challenge in each is what I find interesting. Thankfully, I'm a better physicist than I am a musician! But I get joy from both.

[tone]

Part 2

Audio track: FCE_Listening_9_2.mp3

Now turn to Part 2. You hear a man, Paul Oswald, taking about his hobby, wild swimming. For questions 9–18, complete the sentences with a word or short phrase. You now have 45 seconds to look at Part 2.

[tone]

It was shortly after my thirtieth birthday that I began 'wild swimming', by which I mean swimming in natural water – usually rivers or lakes. I realised that I lived in a city, I travelled through the city to get to my office, which was also in the city, and I never saw the countryside! I couldn't remember the last time I'd been on a walk or climbed a tree, so I think I was ready to get involved with the great outdoors. And when a friend suggested a day trip to go wild swimming, I thought 'why not?'

That first swim wasn't a great success, as it happens. It turned out that we hadn't checked the weather forecast beforehand: It was cold for that time of the year – really cold – and it rained solidly all day. If I remember rightly, we spent several hours walking through a muddy forest to get to the lake, and I managed to cut my hand badly on the way back. The swim itself lasted no more than ten minutes, but what a memorable ten minutes! Swimming in natural water is nothing like the boring mechanical swimming you do at the local swimming pool: I felt connected with nature and soon I was swimming every chance I got.

There's nothing quite like splashing down a river, watching shoals of fish swim around you in the clear water, exploring under overhanging trees or through beds of reeds. My personal favourite is to swim from the mouth of a river into a lake I've found – I'm not going to tell you where it is: I think of it as my own private spot. Once I'm in the lake itself, there's a little island where I like to sunbathe on a big flat rock. It's like being king of the river: I love it!

To begin with, I worried a little bit about safety, but as I gained experience I've come to know what to look out for. I advise new wild swimmers to build up very slowly and not go out too far to begin with. A rule of thumb I've heard is to limit yourself to ten percent of your indoor swimming range until you have got used to wild swimming. Cold is the biggest problem: even in the summer, open water can be chilly, and deeper water can have layers of extreme cold below the surface, which can cause trouble. And, of course, you have to look out for weeds and for river traffic.

Okay, so, some top tips for a successful wild swim: First of all, try to pick somewhere that's easy to get to and has convenient parking nearby. That might sound very 'un-wild', but remember that you're going to want to get dry very quickly after the swim, and you might not want to walk miles back to your car. And look for somewhere with a nice picnic spot nearby – it always helps me when I'm swimming to have a good lunch to look forward to afterwards.

And if you don't want to swim alone, there are clubs and societies all over the country. There are even mass-swims with hundreds of people you can go on. I haven't tried that, myself, as I prefer doing it in smaller groups, or in my own company, but the most important advice of all is to give wild swimming a try as soon as you can. There's nothing quite like it for connecting with nature and for washing off the dust of urban life.

[tone]

Part 3

Audio track: FCE_Listening_9_3.mp3

Now turn to Part 3. You hear five people talking about buying a home. For questions 19–23, assign the correct speaker to the statement given. There are three extra options which you do not have to use. You now have 30 seconds to look at Part 3.

[tone]

Speaker 1   Yes, it is stressful, but so are many things in life. My husband gets a bit bored, I think. I drag him round so many potential new homes, and, if I'm honest, I know I'm not serious about buying most of them, but I get a real kick out of seeing how other people live. My husband says I'm nosey, but I'd say I'm 'inquisitive'. And, even when we have no intention of moving, I sometimes stop to look at showhomes on new estates. I'm addicted!

Speaker 2   I know everyone needs to go through it at some point, but, honestly, it's a ridiculous process. You'd think they would find a less painful way, seeing how everyone does it. First, it's finding the place, then all the checks that need to be done – and dealing with those estate agents is like pulling teeth! Everyone wants money from you, and everyone needs everything done 'yesterday'. I actually went to the doctor once because it was making me feel so bad. I have a reasonably responsible job, and two kids to look after, but nothing compares with buying a house.

Speaker 3   It's the third house we've had now, and it was our choice to move to this smaller bungalow – you know, with us getting older and all that. The kids have flown the nest long ago, so we didn't need five bedrooms anymore. It's expensive to move, of course, with all the agent's fees and taxes, but with the money we made off the old house we have a nice little sum now for our pension. We'll see out our days here, I hope: it's a lovely house to spend our retirement in.

Speaker 4   Our business is Property: we buy houses and live in them while we're doing them up before selling them. It's been more difficult recently, though, with the housing crisis, and we're not able to sell this one as quickly as we'd like to. It means we just have to wait until this one sells before we move on. It's as simple as that. No problem, really. I have another job and I work from home on the internet, so that keeps us fed, but as soon as someone does buy this house we'll be on to the next project.

Speaker 5   I'm the interior designer of the two of us and leave everything else to my wife. She has always decided on the house in our four previous purchases, and I learned straight away that it was just easier to keep my mouth shut when she is looking. She knows our budget – and you'd better believe she'll spend every bit of it – so there's no chance of us saving money. If I did offer my opinion back then, she'd never listen to me anyway, and at the end of the day, if she's happy, so am I.

Part 4

Audio track: FCE_Listening_9_4.mp3

Now turn to Part 4. You hear an interview with Annie Williams, who has always dreamed of being a writer. For questions 24–30, choose the best answer, A, B or C. You will now have one minute to look at Part 4.

[tone]

Interviewer: So, Annie, you've just published your tenth fantasy novel. And it's brilliant. Tell us how you came to get your dream job.

Annie: Okay. To begin with, like most fantasy authors, I was a fan: I grew up reading fantasy novels and watching every movie that came out, but I went one step further than that. I began going to conventions and building up a network of friends who were into the same things as me. There are a lot of very committed fans out there, who think nothing of queueing for hours on end, just for their favourite author to sign their copy of the latest bestseller. That was me!

Interviewer: But not many fans get to be a writer themselves ...

Annie: Well, you'd be surprised, actually. I know dozens of people who have published their own stories: there are so many platforms to be creative on nowadays. Some of these people have even produced full series of books, and had them printed themselves. Of course, the quality is very variable, but if you spend a bit of time googling you can find some extremely imaginative fiction, every bit as good as mine.

Interviewer: So, do you think you just got lucky then?

Annie: Hmm. I suppose there's a little bit of that. I'm not saying I'm no good, but I'm sure there are better writers who will never be discovered. ..... Actually, when I come to think of it, it wasn't just luck: all that time spent going to conventions meant that I met a lot of the right people. And I set up a blog where I reviewed all the latest fantasy books and interviewed authors – that meant the publishers knew my name, and knew that I understood the business of writing.

Interviewer: The business of writing?

Annie: Of course! Writing is a business. It's not enough just to produce the content. You have to work hard to sell it, too, which, in most cases, means getting out there and selling yourself! I put a lot of work into my website, for example, which means my readers – who, of course, are my customers – always hear about my latest project. That's my most important point of contact with the public. And I travel a lot, too, going to libraries and fantasy conventions to meet readers.

Interviewer: What do you think of the fans? Are any of them, erm, odd?

Annie: Well I am one! A fan, I mean. That hasn't changed. I still watch *Game of Thrones* as avidly as the next fan, and I think maybe people who don't love fantasy think we're all 15-year-old boys with no social life – dressed up as goblins, probably. However, that's a long way from the truth. Just as many women read fantasy as men, and you'll meet people of all ages and from all walks of life at the conventions. There are a lot of people dressed as goblins, though!

Interviewer: We should round-off with a plug for your latest book ...

Annie: Of course! Thanks. That's why I'm really here after all! Well, for those who haven't read any of my books, let me quickly describe them. They're all set in fifteenth-century London, but it's a version of London where they've opened a door to another, magical world. The new book follows a sort of policeman working for Queen Elizabeth, on the trail of a mysterious killer. Like most detectives he has a pretty dark secret himself ...

[tone]

Transcripts

Test 10

Part 1

Audio track: FCE_Listening_10_1.mp3

FCE Academy, listening practice for the Cambridge English First FCE examination. As it is in the exam, each recording will be introduced and you will have time to read the questions before the recording is played. In the exam, you will hear each recording twice. At the beginning of each recording you will hear this sound: [tone]. It is good practice to write notes while you listen to each recording.

Part 1: You will hear people speaking in eight different situations. For questions 1–8, you must choose the best answer, A, B or C.

Question 1 You hear a woman talking on the phone about a missing item from the shopping she has ordered online. How does she feel?

[tone]

Well, I understand you are busy, but it's not really an excuse, is it? I know these things happen, but I took the time to make the order online. The least you lot can do is make sure it all arrives. I promised my grandson his favourite meal for dinner and he'll be so disappointed. It's his birthday, you see. It just really makes me mad: online shopping is supposed to be more convenient. Whatever am I going to do now?

[tone]

Question 2 You overhear two friends speaking about a movie they have just seen. What do they agree on?

[tone]

Woman: Well, I'm not buying it. There's no way it would have happened like that.

Man: Oh, come on! Where's your imagination? It wasn't supposed to be realistic. It was a fantasy movie. Suspension of disbelief and all that? That's why I go to the cinema.

Woman: Well, I suppose so, but it needs to be convincing.

Man: Fair enough. You need to hand it to Jonny Miles, though. He really is the best actor of his generation.

Woman: You've got that right. Just a pity he decided to take a role is this movie.

[tone]

Question 3 You hear a worker talking about his job. What does he say about it?

[tone]

When I was younger I dreamed about having a job that challenged me every day – which would stimulate me mentally, I mean – but the only thing that's hard about my current job is stopping myself falling asleep: it's repetitive and so very dull. And you're sitting at a workbench all day long. One good thing, though, is that I can listen to whatever music I want to while I work – and that is something I really do enjoy about it.

[tone]

Question 4 You hear a woman talking about gaining a place on a university course. What is she doing?

[tone]

Well, I knew the interview had gone well, and the fact that one of the people interviewing me knew my school teachers was a pleasant surprise, but I don't think that's why I got accepted though. I hope not, at least. I think I was just seen as a good fit for the course. I'm so looking forward to getting started. I've been waiting for this for years, ever since I decided this was what I wanted to study. It's a dream come true.

[tone]

Question 5   You hear a businessman calling a businesswoman. What do they discuss?

[tone]

Man: So, Isabelle, we're all set for the 26th of January then?

Woman: Yes, of course, John. Your secretary was good enough to send me an up-to-date agenda and I think it covers everything.

Man: I know you had to change your flight over from Milan to accommodate this meeting, but I'm sure it will be worth the extra time.

Woman: I'm sure it will, too. We do have a lot to get through, though, so let's make sure we don't get bogged down in the nitty gritty of each issue. It's much better to dot the Is and cross the Ts at a later date and just make sure we cover everything required face-to-face.

Man: I agree completely.

[tone]

Question 6   You hear a woman speaking to a sales assistant in a shop. Why can't she have a refund?

[tone]

Woman: I'm not happy. I bought these shoes here because I was told the quality was good and the customer service was, too. To be honest, so far I've found neither point to be true.

Sales assistant: Well, I'm very sorry you feel that way, madam. As I've explained, we have a strict returns policy: if the item is faulty we will replace it. If you decide that you would rather change it for something else we'll exchange it, but you must bring it back within 28 days. You bought these over two months ago – in the store in Halifax.

Woman: Well, I was there for the weekend and they told me I could exchange them in any one of your stores. They haven't even been worn, look!

Sales assistant: That's right, madam, but it still needs to be within the returns period.

[tone]

Question 7   You hear a man making a statement. Who is talking?

[tone]

A member of staff from Darlington High School called for assistance at 10:30am on Tuesday the 28th March. Officers arrived at the scene and found a car had been broken into – the driver's window having been smashed. A statement was taken from the car's owner, a teacher at the school, and, unfortunately, an item of value had been taken from the front seat of the vehicle. This item, a laptop computer, was clearly marked as property of the school. Anyone with information should contact Darlington Station on 01325 4441000.

[tone]

Question 8 You hear a conversation between a salesperson and a customer. What is being bought?

[tone]

Salesperson: One lady owner from new, it's one of the best models and has been well maintained.

Customer: Okay. Does it come with a warranty?

Salesperson: Of course, sir. Three months as standard on parts and labour, and you can extend that if you like for a small additional fee.

Customer: Right. So, what capacity is the drum?

Salesperson: It's a 7kg drum. It has an economy mode, so it's very efficient and almost silent when it's running. And it's the standard size, so it will fit nicely into any fitted kitchen with no problem.

[tone]

Part 2

Audio track: FCE_Listening_10_2.mp3

Now turn to Part 2. You hear Steve Barlow talking about his career as a professional pianist. For questions 9–18, complete the sentences with a word or short phrase. You now have 45 seconds to look at Part 2.

[tone]

I started playing the piano at an early age – I mean, really really early: five, I think I was – and I didn't actually pick up the violin, which is the instrument on which I perform nowadays, until I was about ten. I worked really hard on both instruments all through school, but it's always been the violin that has provided me with the best opportunities to perform. Truth be told, initially I wanted to be a music teacher, having been inspired by my own teachers when I was at school, but I've always had the good fortune to find enough performance opportunities to make a living without having to teach, although I wouldn't rule it out in the future.

I was good, and I played in the school band and in small chamber groups before getting the opportunity to audition for a regional orchestra. From there I was accepted into a junior conservatory and, when I was 16, I made it into the National Junior Orchestra. I've always been lucky enough to have the very best teachers and I attribute my success to the dedication, enthusiasm, and, most importantly, the patience they showed during our classes.

I got a lot of great advice from them and a window into the life of a teacher and performer, and hopefully I can share some of that advice with you now.

First: practise. Good training is essential for any musician, and if you don't do a lot of it before you start working you may find yourself lacking in the real world – a good university course will give you all of those skills. It's important to develop your playing, of course, and to familiarise yourself with an instrument's repertoire, but it's just as important not to neglect core skills, such as Musicianship. Good keyboard skills really do help with this, as they do for composition, and also, if you do go into the classroom – as most musicians should be prepared to do at some point – you'll really benefit by being able to play the piano well.

Second: network. Especially during your time studying, and throughout your career, it's essential to network and therefore build up lots of contacts. So, participate in as many projects as you can, even if they are unpaid, as the people you get to know might be able to return the favour at some point in the future. As a musician, I'm sure you'll have a desire to go to concerts and listen to as much music as possible, but make sure that you do. All too often I see people who work so hard on one aspect of their playing that they neglect the role of being a music fan and part of that community, which is so important to maintain.

Keep studying: continued study is an integral part of being a musician or a teacher. If you're lucky enough to get work as a performer you'll need to allow two–three hours per day for rehearsals or personal practice. Your lifestyle needs to allow for this and you'll need to do your best to remain fit and healthy to keep up with such physical demands.

Lastly, I'd like to tell you about a truly modern phenomenon – so important today – and that is your own image-management on social media. Usually it's only you who is wholly responsible for your personal brand management, so when you do perform make sure you always post to your Facebook or Instagram account. Tell people about all the projects you are involved in, and always be aware of the fact that you are in control of your image and how the world sees you. In the last few years the people who have been best at this digital brand management have been the most successful artists in the business.

[tone]

Part 3

Audio track: FCE_Listening_10_3.mp3

Now turn to Part 3. You hear five people talking about their experience at job interviews. For questions 19–23, assign the correct speaker to the statement given. There are three extra options which you do not have to use. You now have 30 seconds to look at Part 3.

[tone]

Speaker 1   I haven't had too many job interviews to be honest – only two – but I´m happy to say I got both jobs, so I must have done something right. I remember the first one: I took a deep breath before I entered the room and just kept reminding myself of my excellent qualifications and how well I had prepared for the interview. That's my tip – do your research. Look for the job that's right for you, and know your stuff about the type of work the company does. That way you'll be ready for any questions they might have, and confident, before you even start the interview.

Speaker 2   Now I'm not saying it's the only thing, but I think the most important by far is time-keeping, and I'm not just referring to turning up late. While that will surely severely diminish your chances of getting any job, I also think arriving too early can annoy an interviewer. Imagine you have meetings all day in your busy office and you get some potential employee turning up 30 minutes early. You'd need to find somewhere for them to wait, or, worse, feel pressured to change your schedule to suit Mr or Mrs Early! Show you can tell the time at least!

Speaker 3   My mother always told me to dress for the job you want, not the job you have, so I've always put on my best clothes for a job interview – a suit, a shirt and tie – and I make sure my shoes are well-polished. But I found out the hard way that going formal isn't always the best approach to take. I recently went for a job as a lifeguard at my local swimming pool and, although I thought I had done an excellent interview, I didn't get the job. They actually told me I just didn't look the sporty type! So, I suppose common sense is probably a better way forward.

Speaker 4   I remember it clearly – I was only about 16 – and I knew I'd done well in the written test for basic Math and English before the actual interview. However, when they started explaining what was involved in the job I became really worried about whether I actually had the skills required. What I did next was life-changing for me and is something I'd highly recommendable for anyone: I came clean with the two interviewers and told them I really didn't know anything about working in an office, but that I would promise to work hard and remember everything I was taught. I was asked to wait outside and, after a few minutes, Mr Smith and Mr Jones came out and offered me the job then and there. I worked in that same company for my entire working life.

Speaker 5   As an employer I have many requirements for many different jobs. I need people who are efficient, motivated and dependable: people here work shifts, and everyone takes turns working a weekend from time to time. Above all, though, I need people who can change working roles, are prepared to adapt to the changing requirements of the job and can work in the modern working environment. People with those attributes are very desirable in the labour market.

Part 4

Audio track: FCE_Listening_10_4.mp3

Now turn to Part 4. You hear an interview with Charlotte Orwell, who has a peculiar hobby. For questions 24–30, choose the best answer, A, B or C. You will now have one minute to look at Part 4.

[tone]

Interviewer: So, let me get this straight. We've covered many weird and wonderful hobbies on this show, but you have one of the strangest. You collect ... collections?

Charlotte: Yes, that's right. I do.

Interviewer: What on Earth does that actually mean?

Charlotte: Well, it's like this. A few years ago I gave up my day job to devote myself to writing. I published a couple of novels, but they didn't do very well. I was about to give up and go back to work when my publisher suggested I try my hand at non-fiction. They thought I had the right style to produce a book looking behind the scenes at all the different museums in London, and it turned out I loved the work. That mix of research, interviewing interesting people, seeing the collections that the public rarely see – it was wonderful!

Interviewer: So, do you collect museum collections?

Charlotte: Aha ... no. I spent a few days at a postage stamp museum, and there I met a little group of philatelists – stamp collectors. They were such a fascinating bunch of people and so glad to explain their hobby. It was their special vocabulary that got me interested: they measure the edges of stamps with something called a 'perf gauge', and they call a fake stamp an 'album weed'. I decided I'd write my next book about stamp collectors, just to share some of these lovely words with the wider world, but then I got to thinking about all the other collectors out there, and I decided to make the book about them, too.

Interviewer: Okayyy ... so it's a book about collections. How many do you cover in total?

Charlotte: So far I've written five chapters: stamps, butterflies, teddy bears, postcards, and old share certificates.

Interviewer: Old share certificates? Really?

Charlotte: Absolutely. There's a collection for everyone out there. The scripophilists are people who collect share certificates. When you speak to them, you realise they're preserving an important piece of history. Just think about what stocks and shares represent: people making fortunes, or losing all of their money, famous frauds, the stock market crash and the Great Depression. All those hopes and dreams. Important stuff. The collectors can tell you something about every share certificate they own. Of course, they have their own rules: they look for things like the age of the certificate, the quality of the printing, whether or not it was ever owned by somebody famous ...

Interviewer: Right. Okay. From stocks to something less impressive, postcards: I had a box of postcards myself as a child, but I don't think it was a real collection. Was I sitting on a gold mine?

Charlotte: Well, probably not. But guess what? Deltiology – collecting postcards – is the third-most popular type of collecting, after stamps and coins. Myself, I love all the postcards you can buy at the seaside – the ones with the rude jokes – but the most important collectible postcards are the ones showing photos of towns. The ones which are actual photographs are the best – they're called RPPCs – 'Real Photo Post Cards' – and they can get very valuable. However, the most expensive postcards ever are also the oldest: there's one from 1840 that was sent from a writer called Theodore Hook – to himself. It's worth at least forty thousand pounds.

Interviewer: So there's money in collecting?

Charlotte: To be honest, I think all of the collectors I've met spend a lot more than they ever make. The really big money gets spent in the world of art – millions for a Picasso or an Andy Warhol. My stamp collectors are all hoping they'll find a particular one-cent stamp which sold for almost ten million pounds a few years ago. And there are a lot of expensive carpets out there. I'm hoping to see a carpet from the 1700s next week, one which cost a LOT of money. Carpets are going to be the next thing I cover.

Interviewer: I was about to ask, what about you? Have you got any collections?

Charlotte: No! I haven't got the time to do it properly, and I certainly haven't got the space in my house. For now, I'm just going to carry on collecting my collectors.

[tone]

How to download the audio

To download the accompanying audio files, please visit our website:

http://prosperityeducation.net/fce-listening-audio-download

Use the password TIAB to access this page.

The audio file size for all ten tests is approximately 20MB.